**RED GUIDE**

D0580900

# The Cotswolds

## Edited by Reginald J. W. Hammond

*Ninth edition*

WARD LOCK LIMITED · LONDON

This guide covers the Cotswold country, mainly in Gloucester-shire, but also penetrates the borders of Oxfordshire, Wiltshire, Somerset, Hereford and Worcester and Warwickshire, and includes the town of Cheltenham.

© Ward Lock Limited 1974

Reprinted 1977

ISBN 0 7063 5487 7 Paperback

Published in Great Britain by
Ward Lock Limited, 116 Baker Street,
London W1M 2BB, a member of the Pentos Group.

Printed offset litho in Great Britain by
Cox & Wyman Ltd., London, Fakenham
and Reading.

GM

# Contents

3

# THE NORTH COTSWOLDS

# THE NORTH-EAST COTSWOLDS

# SOUTHERN COTSWOLD

# Illustrations

# THE RED GUIDES

### Edited by Reginald J. W. Hammond

## RED TOURIST GUIDES

## WARD LOCK LIMITED

# The Cotswolds

The word "Cotswold" is derived from the Anglo-Saxon *cote*, a sheepfold, and *wold* or *weald*, a piece of open uncultivated land, downs or woods. The area known as the Cotswolds lies in the heart of England, being mainly in Gloucestershire but penetrating the borders of Oxfordshire, Wiltshire, Somerset, Worcestershire and Warwickshire.

In this lovely countryside of wooded hills and open downs were bred, during the Middle Ages, vast flocks of long-woolled sheep, known as the "Cotswold Lions". Their fine wool provided a source of great prosperity to the neighbourhood, and by the end of the fourteenth century the wool industry had become England's most important trade. Today only a very few flocks survive of this famous breed.

The wealth garnered by the merchants of the fourteenth to sixteenth centuries is reflected in the magnificence of the churches, and in the gracious beauty of the manor-houses they built. They were fortunate, too, in having excellent building stone at hand, for a wide belt of Oolitic limestone runs through the Cotswolds. From this fine building stone, craftsmen fashioned the charming dignified buildings in the style now defined as Cotswold architecture. Many of the fifteenth- and sixteenth-century houses, their stone mellowed to a soft yellow-greyness, still stand and delight the eye by their beauty of design and proportion. Happily, the majority of the newer buildings conform to existing styles, and harmonize with the old. As H. J. Massingham observed ". . . The word 'progress', as we understand it, has no meaning at all on the Cotswolds, because, once the right way of building —wall, tomb, church, barn or domestic dwelling—was reached, there was no reason for changing it. That is what is meant by the 'Cotswold style'."

7

## Natural Life

The Cotswold scarp is of Oolitic limestone, so called because it is an aggregation of small round granules rather like fish roe. The woodlands are predominantly of beech, and the lesser flora is also that characteristic of limestone country. In the more open part of the beechwoods, one finds hazel, maple, spindletree, elder, whitebeam, juniper and wayfaring tree; various villages boast of ancient and famous examples of oak, sweet chestnut, and yew. Near Boxwell is a forty-acre wood of box that has existed for seven centuries.

The herbaceous flora of the woodland includes spurge, dog's mercury, enchanter's nightshade, violet, wood sanicle and green hellebore. In the deepest shade below the beech trees are the saprophytic bird's nest orchid (*Neottia*) and the yellow bird's nest (*Monotropa*), and in autumn many fungi.

In the pastures and valleys there is an infinite variety of flowering plants: perhaps the most abundant is the meadow cranesbill. Orchids are plentiful—the common helleborine (*Epipactis*), the white and the rarer narrow-leaved helleborine (*Cephalanthera spp.*) and many others. Among unusual finds are the pasque flower (local, but abundant) and the martagon lily (local and rare).

The animals of the Cotswolds are those of normal unspoilt country. Badgers, otters and adders are not infrequent, but the red squirrel has given place to the grey.

Among the many birds to be seen in the Cotswolds one may mention plover, linnet, tree-pipit, whinchat, wagtails and warblers. Less commonly seen are shrike, wryneck, nightjar, nightingale, woodpeckers (green and spotted) and gold-crested wren. Sometimes in spring the corncrake may be heard.

# APPROACHES TO THE DISTRICT

## Railway Routes

From Paddington, the main line which avoids the Severn Tunnel runs by way of Swindon, Stroud and Gloucester. Another line runs through Oxford, Kingham and Moreton-in-Marsh to Worcester.

From the north, the Cotswolds are approached *via* Birmingham to Cheltenham or Gloucester.

For fares, times and details of the various special facilities available, inquiry should be made at any Western Region station or office.

## Roads and Road Services

The shortest route from central London to the Cotswolds is *via* Oxford, Witney and Burford. From south-west London a quieter and pleasanter route is *via* Hampton Court, Chertsey, Ascot, Henley and Abingdon, thereafter branching either to Witney and Burford, or to Faringdon and Fairford.

The Cotswolds are well served by long distance coach services (*see* p. 49 *under* Cheltenham). In addition the whole area is traversed by a network of local bus services, much augmented since the closure of various branch railway lines.

Among the major roads covering the Cotswolds are the following:

A40   Witney–Burford–Northleach–Cheltenham.
A46   Broadway – Winchcombe – Cheltenham – Stroud – Nailsworth–Sodbury.
A429  (Fosse Way) Moreton-in-Marsh–Stow-on-the-Wold– Northleach–Cirencester.
A417  Gloucester to Cirencester, then leaving the Roman Ermin Street and running eastward to Fairford and Faringdon.

## Air Services

Between Gloucester and Cheltenham is Staverton airport, maintained jointly by these two towns. Independent airline companies operate scheduled services to Jersey, Guernsey, Ostend, Isle of Man and Scilly Isles. Charter services to all parts and pleasure flights affording fine views of the Cotswolds, Severn Vale and local beauty spots are also available.

# Hotels and Accommodation

In the larger centres the accommodation is good, and there are hotels to suit various tastes. There are innumerable inns in the villages at which it is a delight to stay. Appearances should not be taken too much into account, for many of the humble-looking establishments can supply first-rate fare and comfort. As far as possible inquiries and reservations should be made in advance. In the following lists the number of bedrooms at the various establishments is indicated in brackets.

## HOTELS

### Bibury

Swan (23)
Bibury Court (15)

### Bourton-on-the-Water

Old New Inn, High Street (18)
Old Manse, High Street
Mouse Trap Inn, Lansdowne

### Broadway

Lygon Arms (54)
Broadway, The Green (13)
Swan, The Green (10)
Farncombe House (19)
Dormy House, Willersley Hill (20)
Crown and Trumpet
Coach and Horses
Inglenook Guest House

### Burford

Bull, High Street (15)
Bay Tree, Sheep Street (24)
Lamb, Sheep Street (14)
Corner House, High Street (9)
Winters Tale (8)
Golden Ball (5)

### Cheltenham

Queen's, Promenade (71)
Berkeley, High Street (50)
Lilley Brook, Charlton Kings (35)
Majestic, Park Place (60)
Moorend Park, Charlton Kings (25)
Carlton, Parabola Road (49)
Savoy, Bayshill Road (59)
George, St. George's Road (46)
Plough, High Street (59)
Irving, High Street (51)
Hollington, Hales Road (7)
Askham Court, Pittville Circus Road (31)
North Hall, Pittville Circus Road (17)
Overton, St. George's Road (25)
Manchester, Clarence Street (33)
Lansdown, Lansdown Road (13)
Wellesley Court, Clarence Square (20)
Carr's, Clarence Street (18)
Rossley Manor Country Club, Andoversford
Golden Valley, Staverton (103)
Aconbury, 16 Bath Parade (13)
Willoughby House, Suffolk Square
The Square Guest House, Suffolk Square
Morville Guest House, 18 Bath Parade

## Chipping Campden

Noel Arms (16)
Cotswold House, Market Square (18)
King's Arms, The Square (10)
Lygon Arms, High Street
Seymour House, High Street (10)

## Chipping Norton

Crown and Cushion, High Street (11)
White Hart, High Street (14)
King's Arms
Fox, Market Place (9)
Bunch of Grapes
Unicorn
Blue Boar

## Chipping Sodbury

Cross Hands (14)
Grapes (6)
Portcullis, Horse Street (5)

## Cirencester

King's Head, Market Place (62)
Fleece, Dyer Street (20)
Crown, West Market Place (14)
Stratton House (20)
Arkenside Guest House, Lewis Lane (16)
Raydon Guest House, The Avenue (10)
Wimborne Guest Arms, Victoria Road (6)
Rivercourt Guest House, The Beeches
    Road

## Dursley

Prince of Wales, Berkeley Road (9)
Old Bell, Long Street (8)

## Fairford

Bull, Market Place (14)
George
Hyperion House (14)

## Lechlade

New Inn, Market Place (17)
Swan
Trout
Crown

## Malmesbury

The Old Bell, Abbey Row (25)
King's Arms, High Street (8)
George, High Street (8)
Stainsbridge House, Gloucester Road (12)

## Minster Lovell

Old Swan (9)

## Moreton-in-Marsh

Manor House (22)
Redesdale Arms (9)
White Hart Royal, High Street (23)

## Northleach

Wheatsheaf (9)
Union

## Painswick

Falcon (6)
Gwynfa (14)
Byfield Guest House (11)

## Stow-on-the-Wold

Talbot, The Square (16)
Unicorn (20)
Fosse Manor (18)
Parkdene (9)
Wyck Hill House (8)
King's Arms, Market Square (8)
Stow Lodge (18)

## Stroud

Imperial, Station Road (24)
Bear Inn, Rodborough Common (32)
Railway, Russell Street
Swan, Swan Lane
Stratford, Beeches Green (12)
Greyhound Inn, Lansdowne
Forester's Arms Inn, Russell Street
Ye Old Painswick Inn, Cirencester Street
Elms Guest House, Beeches Green

11

## Stroud—*continued*

Downfield Guest House, Caincross Road (9)
Laurels Guest House, Stratford Road

## Tetbury

Talbot, Market Place (7)
Snooty Fox, Market Place (10)
Ormond's Head, Long Street
Hare and Hounds, Westonbirt (26)
The Close, Long Street (10)

## Winchcombe

George Inn, High Street (10)
White Hart
Bell Inn

## Witney

Marlborough, Market Square (12)
Fleece, Church Green (15)
Cross Keys, Market Square

## Woodstock

Bear, Park Street (15)
Marlborough Arms, Oxford Street (12)
Dorchester (16)
Woodstock Arms
King's Arms (7)

## Wotton-under-Edge

Swan, Market Street (12)
Falcon, Church Street (5)
Rum Inn, Potters Pond

---

## YOUR HELP IS REQUESTED

A GREAT part of the success of this series is due, as we gratefully acknowledge, to the enthusiastic co-operation of readers. Changes take place, both in town and country, with such rapidity that it is difficult, even for the most alert and painstaking staff, to keep pace with them all, and the correspondents who so kindly take the trouble to inform us of alterations that come under their notice in using the books, render a real service not only to us but to their fellow-readers. We confidently appeal for further help of this kind.

THE EDITOR

WARD LOCK LIMITED
   116 Baker Street
      London W1M 2BB

# Central Cotswold

## Witney to Cheltenham

Coming from London and following the road from Oxford to Cheltenham, one first becomes aware of the Cotswolds as Witney is approached. The change in the scenery is slight enough, but once the flat valley of the Evenlode is crossed the hills become sharper again, kindly stone walls serve instead of hedges and bricks and mortar, while ugly slate roofs are replaced by the lichened stones which are everywhere so characteristic of the Cotswolds.

## Witney

Access.—Buses and coaches from Oxford, London, Cheltenham, etc.
Distances.—Burford, 7 miles; Northleach, 17; Cheltenham, 30; Oxford, 12; London, 68.
Early Closing.—Tuesday.
Hotels.—*See* pp. 10–12.
Parking.—Free car park in town centre.
Population.—13,220.
Sports.—Bowls, cricket, putting, tennis on the Recreation Ground by the Leys.
    Fishing in Windrush and Thames.
Swimming Pool in River Windrush.

The streets of Witney (Oxfordshire) reflect its position as one of the Cotswold border towns. Here and there are buildings in characteristic style, with dormer windows, stone roofs and well-proportioned windows having dripstone courses over them, but there is little of the uniformity that one meets within the district —a uniformity of feeling rather than of style, as is exemplified at neighbouring Burford. Witney is a busy market town with wide streets, good hotels and bus and coach services. Near the top of the main street, among modern-looking shops, one comes across a relic of the days when Witney market was of wider importance

13

—the **Buttercross**—a low building resting on thirteen round pillars. The old Market Cross may have been the central pillar which appears to be much older than the others. The clock tower on the steeply-sloping roof is a much later addition erected in 1683. From the Buttercross a pleasant green extends to the southern end of the town where stands the **Parish Church**. Under the shadow of the great steeple one approaches the Norman north porch. The north transept has a fine seven-light window (this suffered some damage in World War II) and some mortuary arches. Originally these led to a crypt or undercroft, but access to this has been blocked. The small opening in the west wall of the transept is the entrance to an aumbry, five feet long—the cupboard for storing valuable vessels.

In the east wall of the south transept are a blocked arch and doorway which formerly led to a chapel, but the best feature of the transept is the altar tomb with brasses of the Wenman family. The Wenman Chapel, however, is at the north-west corner of the church, divided from the nave by an ancient wooden screen: now used as a vestry, it contains little of interest. Before leaving the church, note the various niches, the unusual spire lights, the corbels in the north transept and the "Pilgrims' Crosses" on each side of the north door.

Other buildings of interest in Witney are the fine Grammar School—the original part dating from 1663—the beautiful houses near Church Green and the Almshouses at Church Corner, and the **Blanket Hall**. This was erected in 1721 in the High Street at its junction with Mill Street. It has a curious one-handed clock beneath which is the Blanket makers' Coat of Arms.

### Witney Blankets

It is difficult to give any accurate information as to the exact date of the introduction of the woollen industry into Witney. Some authorities state that in all probability the weaving of woollen cloth was introduced into the town about the time of the Romans. The Bishop of Winchester was interested in this trade in the town of Winchester, and as he had a palace and manor in Witney he may have introduced cloth weaving into the town. Certainly from time immemorial the swift-running little stream would serve for water power, so that the industry was likely to centre here. Witney was a very important town in the Middle Ages, sending two of its burgesses to Parliament. The weaving industry in Witney is mentioned in the twelfth century in the accounts of the local Manor Courts.

On several occasions Kings have visited Witney. King John was here frequently, and Henry III, in 1221, visited the Bishop of Winchester at his residence in the town. He is said to have purchased some cloth for his wardrobe at the time of this visit. In 1688 James II came to Witney, and the town authorities presented him with a pair of blankets with a gold fringe. Our present Queen came here and received blankets in 1959. A pair of blankets, embroidered with the town's coat of arms, was also presented to her in 1960 on the birth of Prince Andrew.

## The Blanket Weavers' Company

The Blanket Weavers of Witney were incorporated into a company by Queen Anne in the year 1711. Certain regulations were laid down governing the apprenticeship of youths to the blanket trade, and all blankets had to be taken to the Blanket Hall to be weighed and measured before dispatch. For a hundred years this company did very useful work in maintaining the quality and standard of the Witney products, but with the coming of machinery their rules were found to be antiquated, and the company was dissolved in 1847. The Early family were always closely associated with the company, and when it was finally dissolved it was an Early who purchased the assets and paid the debts.

The power loom as we know it today is a comparatively modern invention, very different from the cumbersome contrivance on which those old Witney weavers wove the blankets that have brought fame to a small country town. These old looms needed two men to work them, and the shuttle was laboriously thrown across from one to the other between the threads of warp. The industry is again on a thriving basis; in addition to the production of 30,000 blankets each week, mattresses, divans and eiderdowns are manufactured. Witney is also noted for its glove industry. In recent years a modern factory for motor accessories, and other light engineering industries have developed at an amazing rate.

Witney is a good centre for excursions. A mile to the southeast is **Cogges**. Here is an interesting group of church, manorhouse and vicarage, all of which show thirteenth- and fourteenth-century work. The church dates from *c.* 1100 when it had connections with the Benedictine Abbey of Fécamp. The south aisle and the font are Norman. The curiously shaped tower was built in the fourteenth century. The manor-house dates from *c.* 1250. It has retained some thirteenth-century windows and there are interesting Elizabethan additions.

Three miles north-east of Witney, the village of **North Leigh** lies just off the Witney–Woodstock road. The church at the foot of the hill has a Saxon tower, a Norman north doorway and the Wilcote chantry Chapel, noted for its fan-tracery roof and fine fifteenth-century glass. Archaeologists will be attracted by the remains of a Roman villa, about 2 miles to the north-east of the village. This was discovered in 1813 and is in excellent preservation, revealing tessellated pavements, large bath, hypocaust, etc.


## WITNEY TO CHELTENHAM

Westward the main road leads to **Burford** (p. 20), **Northleach** (p. 31) and **Cheltenham** (p. 49), with fine widespreading views over the wolds. For a more leisurely and interesting route to Burford, one may leave the main road 2 miles from Witney, turning off to the right, down a narrow road signposted to—


### Minster Lovell

After crossing the bridge over the Windrush, bear right at the *Swan Inn* to the top of the street. There is a small car-park here and cars should be left at this point as there is no convenient turning-place later on. Then keep to the right for the church and the ruins of the manor-house.

**Minster Lovell Church,** with its sturdy tower, is charmingly set on a slight slope just above the Windrush. Before entering it is worth while to walk round the large churchyard for the sake of the views of the venerable building in its setting of trees and with the reconditioned ruin of the manor house beyond.

The most striking features of the interior are the four piers carrying the tower. The two westerly piers are quite detached from the walls of the building, and the two easterly ones are, so to speak, only nominally part of the main east structure of the church. From the doorway a glimpse can be had of the vaulted ceiling and of the alabaster tomb

16

in the south transept which is one of the chief sights of the building. The effigy is that of a knight in plate armour and is a good example of fifteenth-century work, though some restoration has been necessary. It is usually held to represent William Lovell, who built the church and the manor-house. Minster Lovell is a place in which to linger: its atmosphere is admirably summed up in the Latin inscription, also in the south transept, to Henry Heylin, who "after the return of Charles II preferred a quiet and dignified life in the country to the racket and ticklish affairs of Court . . ." Minster Lovell is one of the few churches dedicated to St. Kenelm. There are Mass Dials on the outside of the church.

A path rounding the north-east end of the church leads to the ruins of—

## The Manor-House

(Admission Charge. Open from 9 a.m. weekdays, 2 p.m. Sundays.)

For many years a mass of crumbling walls amid a veritable forest of brambles and undergrowth, Minster Lovell Manor-House is now owned by the Department of the Environment. Until recently it was distinctly more picturesque at a distance, but once again it is a pleasant place in which to loiter, admiring the fragments of decoration which tell of the beauty of the building when first erected by William, Lord Lovell, early in the fifteenth century, and listening for the hardly perceptible sound of the Windrush as it sweeps past its willow-bordered banks. The house is the scene of one of those remarkable legends which scientific investigation so unfortunately fails to support. The story goes that Francis, thirteenth Lord Lovell, fought for Lambert Simnel at Stoke, and only escaped from that disastrous field by swimming his horse across the Trent. Thence, so goes the story, he made for Minster Lovell and hid himself in a secret chamber. Only one person became aware of his arrival and to that same trusted servant fell the duty of feeding and caring for his Lordship. Unfortunately, the trusted servant met with an accident, and his Lordship died of starvation. In 1708 during repairs to the house there was discovered a secret chamber, complete with the skeleton of a man seated at a table with his dog at his feet (both skeletons crumbled to dust on the admission of air to the room). The skeleton was presumably never identified. The ruins of the house are once again sweet and sunlit; there is no trace of the secret chamber nor of the creepy sinister feelings which formerly shrouded the spot.

Before leaving Minster Lovell those interested should see the circular stone dovecot in the farmyard north-east of the church, a picturesque survivor of the hundreds of similar buildings which once adorned our countryside.

17

From Minster Lovell those hurrying westward return to the main road by bearing right up the hill after recrossing the bridge, but the more leisurely road on the northern slopes of the Windrush Valley is much more attractive. Turn right at the *Swan Inn* and at a fork in a few hundred yards go left, and left again in **Asthall Leigh.** A little over a mile farther a road on the left runs down into the valley to the bridge which commands one of the most lovely views in the Cotswolds—that of **Asthall** village. In the foreground the Windrush flows placidly through the meads, beyond which the soft grey houses of the village rise to display the church and the many-gabled manor-house. Asthall Church shows a succession of architectural periods—Norman font and pillars, Early English chancel and windows of various styles. The richly decorated recess in the north chapel contains the tomb of Lady Joan Cornwall, a member of the family that owned Asthall.

In Asthall churchyard one finds those curious tombs, so characteristic of certain parts of the Cotswolds, which may be variously said to represent an altar tomb with a stone roll on top or, more picturesquely, an old-fashioned cradle inverted. The style is a local one found only in certain areas.

The gables of the Elizabethan manor-house (some time the residence of Speaker Lenthall) can be seen from the church, and bearing round to the right one has (if the gates are open) a charming view of the east front of the house rising from its lovely gardens. Beyond the gate the road rises and suddenly displays a long reach of the Windrush valley, with Swinbrook village across the meads on the right.

## Swinbrook

(*Swan Inn*) is quite a considerable village, but it is so scattered along the valley that one is never quite sure that one has seen everything. Whatever else is missed, however, one should see the church, perched well above the village and far more interesting within than the curious treatment of the tower arches would suggest. Swinbrook Church is uncommon in having an east window filled with clear glass, and the effect is excellent, for instead of staring at bad-coloured glass indifferently patterned, one looks out to sky and hills. At least, that is the fortune of those sitting in the nave: those occupying seats on the south of the chancel look across to an extraordinary arrangement of effigies that reminds one of a stonemason's showroom. Swinbrook for generations belonged to the Fettiplace family, influential and prosperous, and in any other place the church would have been filled with large altar tombs with effigies. Swinbrook Church, however, could hardly accommodate a single altar tomb, and so the device was adopted of arranging the effigies on shelves on the chancel wall. There are two recesses, each with three shelves, and each shelf bears the effigy of a Fettiplace, attired in the stiff costume of the times, each reclining on one elbow and looking supremely uncomfortable. There are other monuments, to Fettiplaces and others; a Norman font and chancel arch, and some fine chancel stalls displaying medieval carvings.

Barely a mile westward from Swinbrook, and reached either by a fieldpath leading from the churchyard or by the road on the south side, is the tiny, out-of-the-way church of St. Oswald's, **Widford.** The church is beautifully situated near tall trees, and the inside is extraordinarily appealing in its sheer simplicity.

19

It is quite a small building, divided almost in half by a chancel arch. The nave is nearly filled by a high carved oak pulpit, reached by three stone steps, and perhaps a dozen high-backed pews with doors—all in plain unvarnished wood. Either side of the chancel are small patches of tessellated pavement. This is Roman work, and the church is assumed to have been built on the site of a Roman villa. There are also some interesting wall paintings dating from the fourteenth century; but to all who are susceptible to atmosphere this little building has a charm that is far above the contributions of tesserae and pictures.

From Swinbrook to Burford is again a choice of routes: beside the willow-lined Windrush or over the hill to **Fulbrook.** The latter has the advantage of suddenly introducing one to a full-length view of Burford main street—always a gladdening sight, although for some reason the air of harmony which is so predominant in the Cotswolds has missed Fulbrook, with its strange mixture of ancient barns and unattractive modern buildings. Fulbrook Church has a good roof (note the carved heads) and in the chancel a fulsome epitaph worth reading as an example of the taste of bygone days.

## Burford

Access.—Buses and coaches link Burford with London, Oxford, Witney, Northleach, Cheltenham, etc.
Distances.—Witney, 11 miles; Oxford, 20; London, 75; Cheltenham, 22; Faringdon, 11.
Golf Course.—Club House adjoins main road at top of town.
Hotels.—*See* p. 10.
Museum in Tolsey.
Post Office.—Near centre of town.

The fortunes of Burford have been curiously bound up with the development of transport. Notwithstanding the seemingly obvious advantages of a river-crossing at this point, the ford was of no importance in Roman times: Akeman Street, skirting the Oxford basin as closely as possible, crossed the Windrush at Asthall, to the east, and the Fosse strode imperiously across the wolds by Northleach, 8 miles to the west. In Anglo-Saxon times, however, a new trunk road was opened up and the ford over the Windrush became sufficiently important to be fortified (hence the

name burh-ford) and to give cause for a battle. So, against the ford, arose Burford, and for centuries it was of importance as a junction of the north–south and east–west highways—how important can be judged from the size and number of its coaching inns, though many of these are now converted to other uses. Then came the railway age and the relative desertion of the roads, a period during which Burford drowsed peacefully in its valley.

Today with the vast increase in road traffic it is again a busy junction of ways, and for that reason is a very popular place from which to explore the Cotswolds. The Windrush Valley itself has enough of beauty to keep one occupied for weeks, for the placid stream demands—indeed instils—a similar mood in those who wish to know its banks and its delights. And about and beyond the Windrush are some of the fairest of Cotswold scenes.

Burford was not only an important centre of the wool trade; it was noted for the manufacture of saddles, and this occupation received considerable impulse when Charles II, evacuated to Oxford during the Plague, discovered Burford and attended the Races which used to be held a little to the west of the town and which were only transferred to the course between Bibury and Aldsworth when the Burford course fell under the Enclosure Act.

## Burford Parish Church

Burford Church shows its age in its Norman west door and in the lower stages of its tower; and for evidence of the prosperous Middle Ages it is not necessary to go beyond the very fine south porch, with its niches holding statues (once decapitated by Cromwell) and its fine vaulted ceiling. It is in every way a remarkable building. Originally cruciform, it has been so enlarged and altered by the addition of chapels that one has some difficulty in forming a mental idea of the general ground plan. At the south-west corner, for example, is what is now known as the **Lady Chapel,** but which for so long formed the burial-place of the Sylvester family that it bore their name. Originally, too, it was a separate building, which accounts for the fact that it extends farther west than the nave of the church itself.

Looking eastward from the west end one has ample evidence of the changes which have befallen the building. Facing one is the west wall of the Norman tower, and on it are marks showing how from time to time in its long history the roof of the building has been raised. This eastward view, too, is unusual since the low and narrow tower arches do not afford the customary wide view of the chancel; and if we walk under the tower we find that to support the weight of the heightened tower and the spire it was necessary partly to block up the north and south arches, with the result that from the crossing one enters the transepts through quite narrow apertures.

These things are unusual and make Burford Church a most fascinating building to explore. Immediately eastward of the south porch, for example, is **St. Thomas's Chapel,** reached by steps because it is built over an old bone crypt, and from which a doorway leads to the parvise over the porch. From St. Thomas's Chapel one can look down into the **South Transept,** on the walls of which are boards recording many (and sometimes, to us, curious) bequests to Burford and its inhabitants. In the centre of the transept is a large and well-designed tomb to one of the Leggares, for which

reason the transept is more commonly called the **Leggare Chapel.**
Eastward again is the Bartholomew aisle: all that remains of a chapel
in which so many members of the Bartholomew family were laid to
rest. Many of the monuments bear the fulsome inscriptions common
to the age, but most of them are worth reading. In the Chapel of
St. Catherine is the elaborately magnificent tomb of Sir Lawrence
Tanfield, Lord Chief Baron of the Exchequer to Elizabeth I and
James I.

Formerly a simple stone in the vault below the **North Transept**
marked the resting-place of Speaker Lenthall, but there is now no
mark to record his burial here. So long as English history is taught
there will be memory of his courageous reply to the infuriated
Charles when he entered the House of Commons to demand the five
Members who had dared to defy him, but few know that it was
Lenthall's own wish that his tomb should bear no further comment
than the two words *Vermis sum*—"I am a worm", which, however,
cannot be discovered.

Passing now into the north aisle of the nave we have on the left
what is known as **St. Peter's Chapel,** enclosed in an oak screen, made
up from fragments, mostly fifteenth-century work, found in other parts
of the church. The statue from which the chapel takes its present
name was found in another part of the church but now occupies the
place of honour in the chapel. Alongside the chapel, in the floor of
the central aisle, is a very fine brass to John Spycer and his wife (1437).

In the centre of the north wall is a remarkable monument commemorating an equally remarkable man in the person of Edmund
Harman, who began his recorded life as one of Henry VIII's pages.
Subsequently we read of him as a "packer", which probably means
that he was engaged in Customs duties. But Harman was evidently a
man to seize opportunities, and the story goes that once when the
King was taken ill, and no doctors were available, Harman volunteered
to bleed His Majesty, an operation he performed with such success
that he was made a member of the Barbers' Company. The story may
or may not be true, but the fact remains that in Holbein's great picture
of the Company of Barber-Surgeons Harman is shown in close company to the King. A photograph of the picture has thoughtfully been
placed on the monument, which has representations of Harman's nine
sons and seven daughters. Curiosity is sure to be aroused by the
figures of Red Indians and the strange fruits which are included in the
sculptural decoration of the monument: it is thought they were added
to commemorate discoveries which had then recently been made by
Cavendish, in whose voyages of exploration Harman's brother had
taken part.

The most human touch in Burford Church is the inscription, by one
of Cromwell's prisoners, scratched on the rim of the font:

ANTHONY SEDLEY PRISNER 1649.

According to the Church records, three soldiers were shot and

23

buried on 19th May 1649, but Anthony Sedley was not one of these, since another entry records that he was forced to watch this execution.

Adjoining the churchyard on the south are the **Almshouses**, founded, as an inscription tells us, in 1457 by Richard Earl of Warwick—the Kingmaker. Facing the Almshouses, and incorporating the old Town Hall, are the buildings of the **Grammar School**, founded in 1571 for boys by Simon Wisdom. Since then the school has become co-educational and has additional modern premises to the south of the Oxford-Cheltenham road.

The name of Wisdom (or Wysdom) is an important one in the annals of Burford and is known to most visitors on account of the carved stone on the delightful house beside the bridge:

SYMON WYSDOM ALDERMAN
THE FIRST FOVNDER OF THE SCHOLE
IN BVRFORD GAVE THES TENEMENES
WYTHE OTHER TO THE SAME SCHOLE
IN AN 1577 AND NEWLY REEDYFYED
AND BVYLDED THE SAME IN AN 1576
ALL LAWDE AND PRAYSE BE GEVEN
TO GOD THER FORE    AMEN

Standing in one of the recesses on the picturesque old bridge, many will recall that hereabouts stood "Plasher's Mead", in which so much of Compton Mackenzie's *Guy and Pauline* was enacted. Though the sentiment of the story may not appeal to everyone, the book can be recommended for its pictures of the Windrush and of Burford generally.

Almost every house in Burford has a history. Just above Wysdom's is the old Vicarage, a lovely building which is certainly earlier than the 1672 carved on the front. Further up is the **Methodist Chapel**, its pillared classical front almost as surprising before a Methodist building as among the homogeneous inns and cottages of Burford. The explanation of its style is that it was originally a private residence. Another fine old building—The Great House—stands in Witney Street. With few exceptions Burford shows an almost complete regard for local traditions. However one misses the uniformity of design which is so apparent elsewhere in the district, one cannot fail to be charmed with the endless variety with which the local style is adapted: no two buildings are alike, yet each harmonizes with its neighbour, and merely to walk up and down the High Street is a rich experience.

**Burford Priory**, for many years a ruin, has been restored and is now occupied by an Anglican community for women. The mansion occupies the site of the thirteenth-century religious house from which it takes its name.

The Priory of St. John at Burford ended with the Dissolution, its stones being sold to Edmund Harman, the King's Barber-Surgeon (*see* p. 23), who presumably built the Elizabethan residence now before us. Sir Lawrence Tanfield (p. 23) then acquired the property and from him it passed *via* Lord Falkland to Speaker Lenthall and the Lenthalls held it for about two hundred years. Here came Queen Elizabeth I, James I and William III, and in view of the frequency of their visits to Burford probably both Charles I and II knew the Priory. The mansion became untenanted and neglected, but was restored during the present century. During the Second World War soldiers destined for Arnhem were billeted here; a plaque in the chapel pays tribute to their heroism.

## Wychwood Forest

Burford is a good place from which to visit what is left of the Forest of Wychwood, now a National Nature Reserve. It is one of the five forests recorded in Domesday and formerly so full of deer that it used to be said of Burford people that (thanks to poaching) they ate in a week as much venison as a London Alderman had in a year. Burford folk long enjoyed the right of hunting in the forest on one day of the year, but this in due time was replaced by the gift of two deer to the town, the venison forming the principal course at a ceremonial dinner in the Town Hall (now incorporated in the Grammar School). Wychwood Forest, however, has shrunken sadly since the days when it extended as far west as Burford and even (so it is said) Bourton-on-the-Water, but the roads between Leafield and Charlbury reveal many traces of indubitable forest, though most of it is now in private hands. It was, indeed, the Enclosure Act which spelt the doom of the Forest as such. Read what H. J. Massingham has to say in *Wold Without End*.

Up to 1863 its dimensions extended from Swinbrook and Woodstock, below Finstock, to north and west of Charlbury. In far more ancient days it reached beyond Rollright, in north-east Cotswold, but the enclosing of its more southerly range did not begin until the mid-Victorian period. Thousands of its great trees were felled, thousands of acres of heath and copse grubbed up and fetched under the plough, so that in a few years all but the present remnant was uprooted. Nor have the results of this savage spoliation been even economically productive, and Arthur Young, who originally advocated it early in the nineteenth century and ought to have known better, proved to be a false prophet. . . .

Four miles from Burford on the Chipping Norton road, the hilliness of which gives good views, is **Shipton-under-Wychwood**, an extensive and quietly pleasant place with but few signs of the hectic days when it was invaded for Wychwood Fair. It is perhaps less truly Cotswold than many villages around: and its truest features are the larger houses at the western end, particularly the lovely Court, with its trim yews, and the *Shaven Crown Inn*— an old building which has been skilfully reconditioned.

The church lies below the village, among sheltering trees, above which it raises its tower and spire, rather overpoweringly decorated with stone footballs. Of the many notable features inside the church none is more appealing than the charmingly intimate little monument to the right of the altar, showing an unknown man and his wife and their four children, of whom two are shown in their cradles. More often noticed is the palimpsest brass which is now mounted in a hinged frame on the wall of the south aisle.

The pulpit and the font are fifteenth-century and carved from single blocks of stone: the latter shows the bear and ragged staff which were the arms of Warwick the Kingmaker, but possibly a more memorable, because more intimate, personal association is that with John Foxe, who is said to have prepared the English edition of his *Book of Martyrs* while acting as clergyman here.

**Ascott-under-Wychwood** (*Churchill Arms* and *Swan Inn*) has a small church with a tower capped with a diminutive bell-cote supporting a wholly disproportionate weather cock. The church has been rather rigorously restored, but is worth seeing. In a window-bay of the sanctuary is the sedilia characteristic of these parts, and on the north wall, opposite the pulpit, is an inscription which must have provided many a preacher with his text:

> She is gone
> But who can tell her worth?
> Think all a woman ought to be
> And she was that.

The brass candelabra remain from the days when the evening services were conducted by candlelight.

What is left of Wychwood Forest is well seen from the road from Ascott to Leafield, going south-east from Ascott to the Charlbury–Burford road and there turning right and then left (the road up from Ascott continues as a bridle path across the fields to Leafield, but is not such a good walk as the roadside). Past the road dipping down to Chilson and Pudlicote we come close to the edge of the trees and scrub, and then can turn between gateposts on the right into the road which for some way is an avenue through what is left of Wychwood Forest. Woods border the road most of the way to Leafield (*Fox Inn, Old George Inn, Potters Arms Inn*), a straggling upland village. Leafield Church is modern and imposing. Near the village is a P.O. radio station.

Eastward from Leafield the road skirts the southern edge of the forest of today; then, reaching the Witney road, our way bears north. **Finstock** hides itself below the road on the right, and then something is seen of Cornbury Park on the left. The mansion (*private*) here dates from the fifteenth century. It contains the room with bed in which Elizabeth's favourite, the Earl of Leicester, died.

**Charlbury** (*Bell, Bull, White Hart* and other inns) is an attractive little town on the Evenlode river, with groupings of eighteenth-century domestic architecture. There is a small museum, and the Meeting House (1779), now business premises, is a reminder that Charlbury was once a Quaker stronghold. The *Bell* (1700) is an old coaching inn. At the lower end of the market-place is the church, outwardly attractive but inwardly much restored. On a buttress outside the south aisle is a painted sundial, and at the entrance to the chancel a tablet by the pulpit commemorates Dr. Ralph Hutchinson, Vicar of Charlbury (1593–1606), President of St. John's College, Oxford. It was, however, a different Charlbury Church he knew: a church of which the wooden circular staircase in the tower and the replaced brass in the south wall are but faint hints.

27

# The Windrush Valley

## Burford to Windrush

The Valley between Burford and Minster Lovell has been described on pp. 17–20; now we follow the stream westward towards its source. As far as the Barringtons (about 3 miles), there are two roads. That beginning at the northern end of Burford Bridge is the one usually followed by motor traffic, but except for the surface the road turning out of Sheep Street about three-quarters of a mile from Burford Tolsey is to be preferred: there is much less traffic and the views across the valley are more extensive since they are not cut off by a continuous ridge of high ground like that along which the Cheltenham highway runs.

On the other hand, the more important Windrush road passes through **Taynton,** and Taynton is not a place to be missed. It is a place of trees and roofs: the church is beautifully set beside the delightful manor-house and well-kept farm buildings, and beyond the trim path leading to the church the road bends to display the main part of the village, which is laid out on the hillside at such an angle that from the crossing one has an unforgettable vision of pure Cotswold roofs—and to those who love the Cotswolds few sights are more satisfying. Taynton stone, by the way, is a famous building material. Blenheim Palace is built of it, and it was used in a number of Oxford colleges.

Between Taynton and Barrington one looks down on the meads through which the Windrush steals in summer and over which it floods in winter.

**Great Barrington,** on the Windrush, consists of a small village, a church of Norman origin, but much restored in 1873, and the large wooded estate of Barrington Park. This great deer park with magnificent trees and fine herds of deer is surrounded by a high stone wall which secludes Barrington Park House—a mid-eighteenth-century mansion with later additions.

Until 1734, the estate was owned by the Bray family, and the chief feature of interest in the **Church** is the five sculptured memorials to the Brays. Near the font is a particularly beautiful mural monument to two children, Jane and Edward Bray. It is believed to be the work of

28

Francis Bird, who sculptured the monument in St. Paul's Cathedral to the daughter of his friend, Sir Christopher Wren. Squeezed between the organ and the north wall is a monument of a different type but having its own interest, for it represents Captain Edmund Bray, wearing Tudor ruff and armour but carrying his sword on his *right* side. The popular explanation of this peculiarity is that the Captain killed a man, was pardoned by Queen Elizabeth and vowed that in contrition for his crime he would never again use his right hand. Other and possibly simpler explanations will occur to the reader; but the Elizabethan legend is worth preserving.

From Great Barrington the road runs swiftly down to the Windrush. Beyond the bridge the Sherborne road goes to the right, but before turning in that direction we may diverge a little to the left and inspect **Little Barrington,** which is spread out along the sides and head of a little irregular combe running down to the Windrush. Towards the top of the hill the road to Burford by the south side of the valley (*see* p. 28) comes in, and a hundred yards or so along this is the church of Little Barrington.

It is of an appealing simplicity. East of the nave is a small Sanctus bell-cote and at the west end a low tower. The church, entered by descending steps and a good Norman door, has a north aisle divided from the nave by two Norman arches on low but sturdy piers. The chancel is very narrow—but indeed the whole building teems with interest for those who love old churches. (Visitors should not overlook the Norman tympanum built into the north wall and the curious sculpture in the porch wall commemorating William Taylor and his family.)

From Barrington to Windrush is a matter of little more than a mile along a tree-shaded road affording lovely views across the valley to Great Barrington House in its fine setting of trees and lawns.

The hamlet of **Windrush** appeals on account of the happy way in which it is spread out on the hillside just above the point where the Windrush stream changes its course from south to east. It is quite small and almost the only outstanding feature is its church, which has a very fine Norman doorway with a double row of demon's beaks. The interior displays a wealth of bold carving. There are scratch dials on the south transept and by the south entrance. The church, with its white walls and clear glass, is light and pleasing. Note the mounting block by the churchyard gate and the curiously carved tombs.

Here our road leaves the River Windrush, which comes down from the north by Bourton-on-the-Water (described, with the Rissingtons, on other pages—*see* Index), and we follow the tributary which comes down by Farmington and **Sherborne.**

Sherborne Manor at one time belonged to the abbots of Winchcombe, who were frequent visitors. The present mansion was built about 1830 and stands in a park of 300 acres, bounded by a high wall. Now an educational institute, the grounds are open on written application. The village consists mainly of pairs of cottages straggled along the road. With their stone roofs and dormers, these are in the purest Cotswold tradition, and they are every bit as beautiful as the more famous Arlington Row at Bibury; but instead of a stream they look out upon long front gardens of the true country type. The church of St. Mary Magdalene was rebuilt in 1850, except for the tower and broached spire which are unusual in this part of the country. It is chiefly of interest by reason of its monuments: in the chancel are two by Rysbrack and Westmacott respectively—note the very unusual alteration in the name of the person commemorated by the former. On the nave walls are many memorials of the Duttons, who, as one reminds us, descended from Odard, a companion in arms of William the Conqueror. One wonders whether Odard had a hand in the building of the church of which the only surviving relic appears to be a well-carved Norman doorway which is now built into a cottage at the extreme eastern end of the village. From the neighbourhood of Sherborne House there are good views across the valley, the floor of which is covered by a large lake formed by damming the Sherborne brook as it comes down from Farmington to join the Windrush.

Beyond the next crossways the surface of the road we are following deteriorates and becomes a country lane, winding delightfully along the hillside and up through woods to **Farmington** (*see* p. 100). Less than 2 miles from Farmington is **Northleach,** which is more directly reached from Witney and Oxford by the busy main road.

## Northleach

Access.—By bus and coach from Witney, Oxford, Cheltenham, Cirencester, etc.
Nearest station: Cheltenham (13 miles).
Early Closing.—Thursday.
Hotels.—*See* p. 11.

Northleach is a former market town which had its beginnings about the year 1230. It was once an important centre for the wool trade and, like other Cotswold villages, was enriched in the fifteenth century by prosperous merchants who endowed fine buildings and a splendid church. A few of the ancient houses can be seen near the Market Place, and in the main street is a row of well-preserved seventeenth-century almshouses. But the glory of Northleach is its magnificent church. Set a little distance from, and conspicuously above the market-place and houses, its dignity is such that entering the town by the busy main road, one has the feeling of coming to a cathedral city.

### Northleach Church

The exterior demands almost as much attention as the interior. From the south-east the grouping is particularly fine. Eastward from the tower, 100 feet high, comes the nave, its roof battlemented and pinnacled, and at the east end the unusual window over the chancel arch. Contrasting with the flattened arch of this window is the pointed roof of the chancel, the range of tall crocketed pinnacles being carried on by those of the south porch, on which is the spirelet over the staircase leading to the parvise. Even from here the beauty of the window tracery can be appreciated.

The most beautiful feature, however, is the **South Porch**, lofty and with the upper part of its front adorned with niches for statues, of which the original figures of the Virgin and Child remain below a canopied statue of the Holy Trinity, but both are

badly weathered. Internally, it is a splendid example of graceful vaulting, and though weatherworn, the details of many of its carvings can still be followed.

The interior gives an impression of lightness and space, partly because of the lack of coloured glass in nave and clerestory and also because of the large and unusual window over the chancel arch. Note the concave octagon pillars of the nave arcades. The rood-loft once extended right across the north side chapel and chancel—the stairway is in the north wall. The north aisle is occupied by the choir and organ. The south choir aisle, or Lady Chapel, is interesting for the T deeply incised* on its west wall, beside the door: this was the mark of the twelfth-century builder of the earlier Lady Chapel and north choir aisle. Note the double hagioscope or squint providing a view of the High Altar and in the chancel the graceful sedilia. The corbel heads in the N.E. and S.E. corners show Henry VII and his Queen, the chapel having been built in this reign. The east wall of the south aisle has a remnant of a fifteenth-century reredos.

Numerous other features demand notice: the aisle roofs, the south aisle being original fifteenth-century work; the carved stone fifteenth-century pulpit; the fourteenth-century font, now back in its original position by the south door, has a bowl supported by angels, the pedestal standing on, and crushing, evil spirits.

The newel stairway from the south aisle of the nave leads to the south porch room, which may have been constructed for the use of a visiting priest. It contains a large fireplace, a baking oven and lamp brackets.

Finally but not least among the points of interest in the church are the very fine brasses, principally of Woolstaplers, hence the representations of sheep and woolpacks. Several of these brasses are well seen, notably that of John Fortey who rebuilt the clerestory; and also the fine brass showing Thomas Fortey with his wife Agnes and her first husband William Scors, a tailor, hence the scissors at his feet. Note also the numerous animals in the border of this brass.

Northleach is very well placed for visiting a number of places of great interest and beauty. A few miles to the south is the **Coln Valley,** with Chedworth Roman Villa (*see* p. 44) and a number of delightful villages; eastward through Farmington one runs down to Sherborne and the Windrush Valley; northward along the

---

* Incised on the S.E. pillar, near the bottom, is the name of Henry Winchcombe, possibly a mason, though a Henrie Winchcombe was vicar from 1556–1560. Numerous fifteenth-century mason's marks include the W of William Nutts and the W of Simon White both of whom also helped to build Chipping Campden church.

Fosse Way to Bourton-on-the-Water and Stow-on-the-Wold and such villages as the Slaughters and the Swells—places which have been more freely quoted as examples of Cotswold beauty than any other. Westward, again, one can pursue the busy main road to Cheltenham or make more leisurely ways through the lanes. A very delightful excursion is that by Hampnett to Turkdean.

At the cross-road at the west end of Northleach turn up by the right at the disused prison and in a hundred yards or so turn off to the left by a road which comes to—

## Hampnett

a handful of barns and houses among which, as the scene unfolds, a church is revealed. Tower and nave date from the fourteenth–fifteenth centuries and are built on to a Norman chancel. Note the birds on the capitals of the chancel arch and the clear-cut moulding over it; the rood-loft stairs and the low vaulted sanctuary roof.

Turning our backs on the busy Oxford–Cheltenham highway, we leave Hampnett and by gracious stone-built farms and barns come out on to the top with a grand and colourful view over the Windrush Valley which is succeeded by a sudden vision (no other word fits the picture) of—

## Turkdean

a poem of quiet grey stone spread on a green hillside. The vision vanishes as the road falls steeply to an orchard, and a few hundred yards farther turns sharply back to the left to take us up through an avenue of beeches, but the scene is as remote from great highways as one could desire. As for Turkdean, let H. J. Massingham speak:

"Turkdean is sliced in half, one at the bottom of its wooded cliff, the other roosting on its crest, and yet fair in mignon gardens. Behind the proper Cotsall Church is a dreamlike vignette of stone-tiled roofs at many an angle and with varied surface and colouring. In the church-yard, where violets are white, the wayfarer is on a level with these roofs whose abutments and slantings compose so treasured a mental etching. . ." (*Wold Without End.*)

33

Beyond Turkdean we who have not to hurry back to the main highway come out by the Notgrove road on to the wolds—nothing dramatic, nothing of which one can "take hold", but such sheer beauty of colour and contour as lifts the Cotswolds high above any other part of Britain.

## Notgrove

"Next Notgrove, two miles distant, takes its name
From nut tree groves, wh: border on ye same."

Thus, at any rate, an old rhyme of which a copy hangs in the church. More correctly, however, the name is derived from *Nata-graef*, "Nata's Trench," though history is silent regarding both Nata and his trench.

A surprising feature of Notgrove is that although it seems to lie among hills, the churchyard has distant glimpses of the Berkshire downs, many miles away. Although cupped among hills, Notgrove lies high—just above the village the road is over 800 feet above sea-level—and the far-extending view is caught by looking down the valley of the pretty stream which after many a turn and wriggle and joining of forces with other similar streams, runs into the Sherborne brook and in due course swells the volume of the Windrush.

Notgrove, notwithstanding its views, has an air of seclusion: the main part of the village is collected round a slight dip in the hillside, and the church occupies another in company with the delightful old manor-house with its arch of trimmed yew trees. The church is of Norman origin, and though considerably rebuilt in the nineteenth century maintains an appearance of antiquity, with its unplastered grey stone walls and the remains of a fourteenth-century stone reredos. In front of the reredos hangs a very fine tapestry depicting Notgrove manor and church. On the outside of the east wall, too, is a ninth-century carving of the Crucifixion and in the south porch a stone coffin and a recess where relics were shown. Ecclesiologists are interested in the ball-flower ornament in the transept window (a rare feature in this district) and other items are the carved pews (ancient and modern) and the early Norman font.

**Notgrove Barrow** lies about a mile from the village, alongside the road to Andoversford, gained by following the left fork on leaving the village. About 200 yards short of the station (closed), on the left, is a farm lane, and the remains of the barrow are in the enclosure in the angle and are now in the care of the Department of the Environment. The barrow has been excavated several times; human skeletons, pottery and other relics have been found.

"About a score of the stones remain, enough to reveal the structure of passage-way, central burial-chamber and lateral transepts as corresponding with the ground-plan of the Twelfth Dynasty Egyptian and Middle Minoan Cretan rock-cut tombs. It lies quite open to the rain and frosts and suns, and, for all the ruin of the mound and dilapidation of the chambers, it is a tomb in the grand style of the cult of the dead."

Eastward of Notgrove is the village of **Cold Aston,** now more often referred to as **Aston Blank** to distinguish it from the village of **Cold Ashton,** four miles north of Bath (p. 147). Turn sharp right on leaving Notgrove village and in just over a mile the long grey street of Aston is seen curving away, and there is a glimpse of the church behind the trees. Cold Aston is an apt name, for the village lies on the high wind-swept hills, unprotected by trees and exposed to bleak winds. There are some attractive old houses, mostly hidden by the protecting tall hedges, and a fine barn used in the sixteenth century as a pigeon-house. The church is of Norman origin, and although restored in 1875, has retained several Norman features. There is a good south door *c.* 1125 and a blocked north door of the same period. There is no east window, but the remnants of a stone reredos over the altar. The chancel is mid-fourteenth century; there are fragments of Norman moulding and other interesting features including an Easter Sepulchre.

**Northleach to Cheltenham.** Climbing the hill out of Northleach, one has a comforting view to the right of Hampnett Church, snugly set among its farm buildings (*see* p. 33); then we settle down to the long gentle winding road over the wolds and past *Puesdown Inn* (840 feet above the sea) and so down to **Andoversford,** and out into the green valley along by **Whittington** (p. 46) and below **Dowdeswell** (p. 45). Then come the reservoirs which herald the approach to **Cheltenham,** which is described on pp. 49–62.

# The Coln Valley

The Coln is a crystal-clear stream rising in the hills near Seven-hampton and making a leisurely and lovely way to the Thames at Lechlade. Almost throughout its course of 25 miles it is typically Cotswold, drowsing in the shade of tall woods, dimpling past sunny meadows and gladdening villages which for sheer unspoilt beauty cannot be matched in any other part of Britain. No one wishing to know the spell of the Cotswolds can omit to visit the Coln Valley, and no one who visits it can fail to be impressed with its quiet beauty. Moreover, it is enriched by three places of outstanding merit—Fairford, with its church full of painted windows; Bibury, that place of grey stone cottages and lurking trout, and Chedworth, the most complete, as the most charm-ingly placed, of all our relics of Roman civilization.

Lechlade, where the Coln waters join with those of the Thames, is a quiet little town of wide streets in the angle of which the church raises its beautiful tower and spire. The beauty of this "aerial pile" has moved others before and since Shelley—seen from across the water-meadows it is one of the loveliest things on the Thames, and one recalls with gratitude that this scene prompted Shelley's perfect "Summer Evening" Meditation.

Though not *in* the Cotswolds, Lechlade is definitely *of* the Cotswolds: apart from details of building, it has that calm and restful air which defies definition or analysis and which breathes over Cotswold as nowhere else in England. It is, however, better known to voyagers along the Thames, being about 40 miles of tortuous winding above Folly Bridge, Oxford, and sufficiently above the often-crowded stream about Oxford to ensure quiet and leisurely boating. It is also a good spot for fishing.

Some 4 miles west of Lechlade is—

# Fairford

**Access.**—Buses from Cirencester and Swindon.
**Bank.**—*Lloyds*, High Street.
**Churches.**—*St. Mary's* (parish church); *Congregational Chapel*, Milton Street.
**Early Closing.**—Saturday; some on Thursday.
**Hotels.**—*See* p. 11.
**Population.**—1,840.

Fairford is an ancient market town on the River Coln, beloved by anglers for its trout fishing. It is famed for the wonderful series of windows in its church. The windows, in fact, are so overwhelming in their claim on our attention that one is apt to forget there are other features of interest, including excellent carved screens. It is to John Tame—that great wool-stapler of the fifteenth century whose tomb is in the chancel—that we owe Fairford Church and its glass. This was apparently made in England especially for these windows, and Tame's general idea seems to have been to make them "a sermon in pictures, like the People's Bible windows in Canterbury", the subjects ranging from Eden to Pentecost, from the Apostles to the Judgment.

But "it is the devils who get all the attention from visitors," remarks Mr. Warren in *A Cotswold Year* (*Bles*). "And no wonder. We all have a hankering after horrors, and horrors here out-Herod Herod. There is one blue devil, with white webbed feet, carrying off one of the damned in a bright yellow wheelbarrow, while a dark green devil prods the cart from behind with a red-hot poker. There is a blast furnace (or glass-maker's oven, to be more precise, for the mediæval artist loved to embody his imagination in the familiar forms of everyday life and work) being blown up by a blue devil, and one can see the lost souls inside, impaled on forks, while the flames lick round them. There is a mill (similar to that in which the glass was ground) with more lost souls thrust into the hopper so that their bones may be crushed as they are drawn down through the revolving cogs into the vat below. There is a crucible filled with molten metal in which the damned suffer, though they never die. But worst of all there is Satan himself, sitting with his hands upon his scaly knees, his long green tail winding about his feet; in his belly is a mouth with two rows of enormous teeth, under a flat nose, and round eyes, brightly staring; and on his shoulders is a fishlike head, with jaws wide open, showing great hooked teeth between which the lost souls disappear amid curling flames.

"With such horrors to see, nobody bothers to look a second time at the procession of the elect winding slowly up the stairs to heaven. Hell is so much more exciting. . . . The fifteenth-century artists who designed

these Fairford windows did their level best with heaven, filling it with the circling Seraphim and Cherubim, ruby and blue; but . . . their heaven is a pale and tame affair compared with their hell, with its hosts of horned devils scuttling away with the damned thrown screaming across their shoulders."

The twenty-eight windows are of brilliant fifteenth-century glass except for three west windows which had some slight restoration in the seventeenth century.

There are some picturesque houses in the village, a half-timbered sixteenth-century house, and a fine old mill on the bank of the Coln. At Keble House, in London Street, John Keble the poet, and one of the leaders of the "Oxford Movement" (*see* p. 48) was born in 1792.

At Fairford we begin to leave the wide meads of the Thames Valley and to get in among the hills. **Quenington,** in this respect, is a charming introduction to the pure Cotswold valley-village: stone-built cottages set about the hillside in flower-gay gardens; larger houses, trimmer and neater, fit into the prevailing harmony.

Quenington has so many attractive houses that one is apt to overlook the **Church** which was originally built in the twelfth century. Its magnificent doors are outstanding even in this district of good door-ways, but the rest of the church has been much altered and now has little to compete in interest and beauty with the two Norman door-ways. Quenington north doorway, now protected by a timbered porch, is richly decorated with deeply cut moulding—all good Norman work—and over it is a tympanum, also Norman, showing the Harrow-ing of Hell: Our Lord is shown piercing Satan, bound hand and foot, with a cross, while suppliant forms, possibly of Adam and Eve and Abel, are drawn from the abyss and the symbolical maw of the whale.

38

The south door is hardly less beautiful in its design: the tympanum depicts the Coronation of the Virgin: the building in the background "might signify either the church or the New Jerusalem."

West of the church is Quenington Court. Here was a preceptory of the Knights Hospitallers: the old gateway facing the road and an unusual circular dovecot (Norman) are the principal remnants.

So far we have seen little of the Coln since we left Lechlade, but in passing from Quenington to—

## Coln St. Aldwyns

there is a sudden and very charming glimpse of it—rather more disciplined than the meandering stream in the Thames meadows, but losing none of its charm thereby. Coln St. Aldwyns climbs the hillside from its mill to its church. Halfway up the main street with several good cottages is the excellent *New Inn*.

The exterior of the church is most pleasing, having the manor-house to one side and the vicarage to the other amid an assemblage of fine trees. Two notable people have been associated with the place: at the beginning of last century the vicar was John Keble, whose son will ever be remembered for *The Christian Year* and who probably first attended service in the church now before us. (The east window commemorates the two Kebles.) In more recent times the manor-house was the home of Sir Michael Hicks-Beach, Chancellor of the Exchequer, and who subsequently became the first Lord St. Aldwyn. The church is worth examining for numerous small details of decoration: high on the outside wall just west of the tower, for example, note the carving of a dragon chasing a man, whom he is about to devour. On the south-west corner of the tower are incised dials and here is a blocked doorway; but the best doorway is that in the south porch—excellent Norman work.

One leaves Coln St. Aldwyns with many a backward look, but there are notable scenes before us. As we travel towards Bibury the Coln is temporarily lost to view—obscured by deeply shelving meadows. Then, with dramatic suddenness, we run down a hill and on the left have a vision of Bibury Court—such a vision as causes the least susceptible of travellers to stop and drink in the scene: the perfect green meadows, short-turfed until they look like lawns, the river sliding gently under the bridge and beyond it the house itself.

## Bibury

**Access.**—By bus and coach from Cirencester, Cheltenham, etc. Bus connections with Western Region at Cirencester.
**Hotel.**—*See* p. 10.
**Population.**—599.
**Early Closing.**—Wednesday.

There are many ways of approaching Bibury, but the best is undoubtedly that by which we have come from Coln St. Aldwyn: it is not merely the suddenness with which the view of the Court and the church comes before us, but the rightness of it: one has the feeling that here is the perfect introduction to an ideal English country village. Bibury repays examination. One walk, for richness of scene, is that along the streamside path from the old mill to Arlington Row and then along by the river to the church. The heavily-buttressed old **Mill** is now a museum (*open daily*). The stone cottages of **Arlington Row** (National Trust—not open), a famous feature of the village, were erected in the fourteenth century and were once used as a wool store. The large field across the road is known as Rock Isle and is where the cloth was hung on racks to dry after fulling.

**Bibury Church** is of Saxon origin. The entrance on the south is Norman. Inside, the walls of the church are lime-washed, a choice of colour that enhances the proportions of the clean and attractive building, emphasizing as it does the slenderness of the chancel arch (original Saxon work) and Norman arcade between the north aisle and the nave, and lighting up the splendid woodwork of the roof. Many other details are of great interest, but most visitors will probably wish to get back to the picturesque village "street" with the Coln running on its parallel course. Here a number of wildfowl are to be seen as also fine specimens of trout. Bibury is always a favourite with anglers. The *Swan Hotel* has a stretch of the stream. In years gone by, too, Bibury was a noted centre for horse-racing: we are told that in the time of Charles II, Bibury, the headquarters of the oldest Racing Club in England, was another Newmarket, and three times the King was here. Indeed, in 1681 the Newmarket Spring Meeting was transferred to Bibury when Parliament met at Oxford.

Half a mile from Bibury is the village of **Ablington**. Here there are some twenty cottages, two farmhouses, a fine barn and two attractive houses—Ablington Manor and Ablington House. Many of its fine trees have now been felled but it remains a quiet and sequestered village of very winding roads.

Now indeed we are in the valley of the Coln: narrow, in places steep-sided, and lined with typical short Cotswold turf studded with fine trees. The road continues to **Winson**, a small village of farmhouses and some modernised cottages. The church has a narrow and lofty nave, from which a depressed Norman arch leads to a diminutive and highly decorated chancel. The effect of these simple ingredients is at least as striking as in many

41

a more elaborate building, and the feeling is heightened by the simple design of the Norman font.

Down by the mill-house we cross the stream and so come to **Coln Rogers.** The second part of the name commemorates Roger of Gloster, a knight who in 1150 gave "Colne in the Hills" (the name is apt now as then) to the monks of Gloucester. Overshadowed by trees, the church is unusually interesting on account of the large amount of Saxon work it retains. In the chancel are several good samples of long-and-short work and a small Saxon window in the north wall; the chancel arch is supported on great jambs of stone almost certainly part of the original Saxon building. The south door is Norman, with a plain tympanum.

From Coln Rogers we come to **Coln St. Dennis,** beautifully set beside the river, its grey old church rising from green lawns, unworried by all the changes and turmoil it has seen since the Normans built its curious tower. This tower divides the nave from the long chancel; the western arch is rounded, the eastern pointed. On the north wall inside the tower notice the curious inscription "HEARE LYES MY BODY FAST INCLOSED WITHIN THIS WATERY GROUND; BUT MY PRECIOUS SOULE IT CANNOT NOWE BE FOUNDE. . . ."

Less than a mile above Coln St. Dennis the river is crossed by the Fosse Way (A429) at **Fosse Bridge.** For a few yards we take this road (to the left), turning off again on the right just above the hotel. In less than a mile a road goes off on the left for Chedworth, but for the Roman Villa keep straight on, over the next crossroads and down to the river, which is crossed at a lovely corner by the woods (see pp. 43–44).


## Chedworth

is a picturesque village spreading over two steep hillsides from which a tributary of the Coln makes a most exciting course from above the church to below the road—here a rippling brook there a fall of quite respectable size, but always hurrying down to the Coln. The best feature of the church is the fine Perpendicular windows on the south side (1490). They are said to have been "originated at the expense of Henry VII, who subsequently reimbursed himself by annexing both church and manor." The nave piers are Norman and so is the font. The stone pulpit is fifteenth-century and, like those at Northleach and elsewhere, it is of the "Gloucester wineglass" type. In the church is a copy of the Geneva Bible, including a plan showing "the situation of the Garden of Eden." There is a good array of gargoyles on the south wall.

The routes leading to the **Roman Villa** are well signposted, but the most direct way for walkers is that through the woods—a distance of a mile and a quarter from the church.

The road from Chedworth to the Roman Villa is that dipping steeply below the old railway and climbing the long hill beyond. From the top of the hill there are far-extending views to the right, and then, as we descend, there are views across the valley of the Coln to **Stowell Park,** at one time the home of the Tames, those great woolstaplers of Northleach. Later it sheltered John Howe the politician who, as Edward Hutton puts it, "cuts such a figure in Macaulay's *History of England.*" In the grounds of the Park is the church, a little Norman gem that should not be overlooked. It is a rare specimen of the latest type of Norman architecture and has some interesting and valuable frescoes, 700 years old, which have been restored recently.

At the cross-roads before the bottom of the valley is reached we turn sharp to the left and join the road from Fosse Bridge on its way down to the river, where we turn sharp to the right and climb up the far side of the valley.

The turning to **Yanworth** with its secluded Norman church prettily placed in a farmyard with Cotswold barns adjacent, is left on the right and we come to one of the fairest scenes in the whole course of Coln. Here is the Cotswold scene in miniature—all the beautifully contoured slopes of short grass, all the graceful groups of trees, everywhere a sense of peace and content. Small wonder that he who built the Roman Villa chose such a site, for the views from its terraced lawns—up to the woods and out across the rolling hills—make one envious of the fortunate custodian of the ruins.

## Chedworth Roman Villa

**Access.**—Though situated in Chedworth parish a mile from the Church, the Villa is more easily reached by way of the Fosse Bridge–Yanworth–Withington road from which there is direct access to the villa.

**Admission.**—*Charge.* The Villa and Museum are open daily, 10–1, 2–6.30 or dusk. Closed Mondays (except Bank Holidays); Tuesdays from October to February inclusive; and every day in January and 1st–15th October.

No villa in the west of England remains so completely exposed to view as Chedworth. The date of the original structure is before the middle of the second century A.D. There is, however, evidence for rebuilding and extension, more particularly in the long northern wing, in the baths at the north end of the west wing, and in the south wing.

The buildings occupy three sides of a rectangular courtyard or parterre; of these, the principal range faces nearly due east, and contains living-rooms and a very complete Roman bath suite. The rooms on the south side, where there was a side entrance, latrine and stewards' room, were built on a slope and on at least two levels, the lower of which probably served as stores or servants' quarters.

The north wing has seen many alterations. It was once composed of two units, a suite of apartments and a large set of baths. When the bath-suite for hot bathing of the Turkish type was built at the north end of the west wing, these original baths were reduced in size and altered so as to form a second bath suite of Swedish type in which dry heat alone was used to promote profuse perspiration, followed by a cold plunge, for which extensive baths were added.

Adjoining the Custodian's house is a museum containing the smaller objects found during excavation of the site in 1864–6. Lord Eldon, the then owner of the property, bore the expense of excavation and built the house and museum and some of the protective coverings over the remains.

The villa became National Trust property in 1924.

Half a mile south-east of the villa is the site of a Romano-British Temple. The site is overgrown with scrub and foliage, but the objects unearthed there are in the villa museum.

Above the Villa the Coln flows between increasingly high hills and as the valley is deeper and narrower so the street of **Withington** seems narrower and more enclosed by high buildings than is usual in such villages, and rather curiously this same air is conveyed by the church, which is entered by a tall well-preserved Norman door while the nave seems unusually lofty owing to the absence of side windows below the clerestory. Two features in the chancel are worth noting: in the north wall is a thirteenth-century pointed window into which has been incorporated chevron moulding from an earlier round arch, and below the window is a small recess made to hold a lead cistern. The cistern has gone, but one can still see the carved stone boss which held the drain-pipe. The cistern was used in connection with the washing of the sacred vessels. By the river just below the church are the *Mill Inn* and the popular *Mill House Restaurant*.

Over the hills north-east of Withington is **Compton Abdale**, with a stream gurgling down its diminutive street and its church raised high on a cliff-like hill immediately above it. Apart from the grey stone of its buildings, the village has more than a touch of Devonshire in its aspect; but the grey stone identifies it as indubitably Cotswold, and the church, though a victim of restoration, has a characteristic north porch, and tower pinnacles in the shape of four dogs.

From Withington the Coln Valley road runs straight as a die towards Dowdeswell, crossing the Oxford–Gloucester road. Those with time to spare are recommended to turn off this road and explore some of the wooded hills to the left of it. There are several prehistoric camps in the neighbourhood, some of which are scheduled as Ancient Monuments.

**Dowdeswell,** from which one looks out across the lake-like Cheltenham reservoir (which looks so very different when viewed from the bordering main road), has a lovely little church (note the dovecots let into the four panels of its tiny spire) neighboured by one of the most delightful of Cotswold houses.

We come under a railway arch to the main road, and for the

sake of the last (or first) few miles of the Coln turn to the right (towards Northleach) for half a mile and then to the left for **Whittington**, which has been described as "an old-world village under a wooded hill". It has kept a fine barn and some of its Tudor houses, but the memorable feature of the place is the situation of the church, which stands on the lawn of Whittington Court, an Elizabethan house restored in 1866.

The church has several interesting features including a Norman north porch, thirteenth- or fourteenth-century stone effigies, a founder's recess in the north wall, and in the churchyard, a fourteenth-century churchyard cross.

From Whittington to **Syreford** (where a Roman site yielded a fine statuette of Mars). A mile above Syreford is **Sevenhampton**, commonly said to be the source of the Coln, though actually it rises farther up the valley: one can trace a stream almost to Charlton Abbots (*see* p. 75). Sevenhampton is in two parts, a handful of cottages on the eastern side of the stream and another handful on the western bank comprising the church, manor-house, etc. The church has many features of interest and beauty, having retained some thirteenth-century work in the chancel and north transept, and an unusual arrangement of the piers and their flying buttresses descending into the middle of the church. There is a noteworthy passage squint from the north transept; the roof is formed of an altar slab.

About half a mile north of Sevenhampton is **Brockhampton**, an attractive village with a fine manor-house set in a magnificent deer park. Here we may leave the Coln, though those who wish to explore its course to the limit can find the tiny brook among the fields between Brockhampton and Charlton Abbots.

(For **Charlton Abbots** and the country on to **Winchcombe**, etc., *see* pp. 75–76.)

A good walk over the hills *via* **Belas Knap** (p. 74) begins by the rough track striking up on the left of the road about half a mile north of Charlton Abbots, opposite Goldwell Farm. Nearing the crest of the hill, the track rounds the end of a wood, and by turning to the right and skirting the upper edge of this wood for half a mile one arrives at Belas Knap.

## THE VALLEY OF THE LEACH

Running more or less parallel with the lower course of the Coln, the *Leach* gives its name to **Northleach** (near which it rises) and to **Lechlade**, where it merges its waters with those of the Thames. The source of the stream is at **Hampnett** (p. 33). A few miles below Northleach the stream comes to **Eastington**, with a church that has several points of interest, though its most important church is the fine building at Northleach, which is actually in the parish of Eastington.

**Aldsworth**, though accounted one of the Leach villages, is actually a good mile from the river. It lies beside the Burford–Bibury road: a kind of backwater, but one worth visiting for its peaceful air and the grace of its Cotswold cottages, set around a hill from which they look across a diminutive valley to the church. Originally Norman, it was largely reconstructed in the sixteenth century, when the fine buttress and the shields and gargoyles above the north wall were added. The church was further restored and enlarged in 1877 but some Norman and Decorated work remains. The twelfth-century oak door on the north side has the original ironwork. The external beauty of Aldsworth Church is enhanced by the lovely old house adjoining. As already mentioned (p. 7) one of the few remaining flocks of genuine Cotswold sheep is to be seen near Aldsworth.

Downstream from Aldsworth the Leach makes a very leisurely and winding course to the twin village of Eastleach: **Eastleach Martin** on the left or east bank, and across the water **Eastleach Turville**, each having a church with Norman work.

The stone footbridge over the river connecting the two parishes is still known as "Keble's Bridge". John Keble (*see also* p. 38) was the minister-in-charge of both churches for eight years and also of the neighbouring church of **Southrop** where he wrote much of his volume of verses *The Christian Year*.

Southrop Church, Norman in origin, still shows Norman work in its north doorway and nicely lozenged tympanum and in its nave, which has some original Norman windows. There are several monuments to the Keble family and noteworthy fifteenth-century effigies to Sir Thomas Conway and his wife, but the most remarkable feature of the church is the tub-shaped thirteenth-century font.

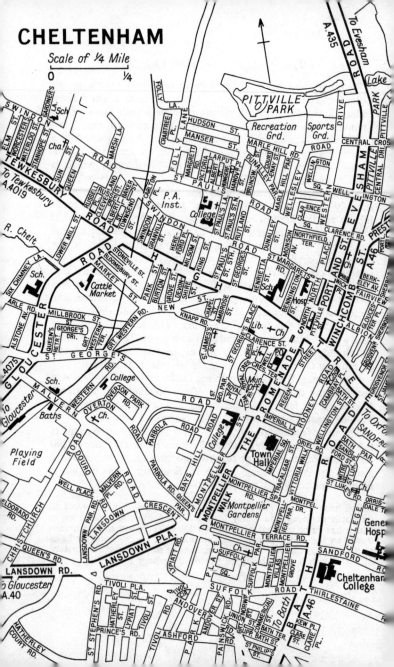

# Cheltenham

## General Information

**Access.**—Cheltenham is centrally situated with railway communication with London *via* Gloucester; the West of England *via* Bristol; South Wales *via* Gloucester and Cardiff; the North and North-West *via* Birmingham.

For distances *see* p. 50. Notes on most of the highways converging on Cheltenham will be found by consulting the Index.

Cheltenham is the central junction of a vast network of coach express services operated under the title of Associated Motorways. Daily services are operated to all parts of the country. *Coach Station* in St. Margaret's Road, a short distance from the High Street. *Country Bus Station* in Royal Well Road.

Air charter services at Staverton Airport, 4 miles.

**Angling.**—The Cheltenham Angling Club have fishing in 11 miles of the River Avon. Day tickets may be obtained from the Bell Inn, Eckington and from the Secretary. A Severn Fishery Authority Rod Licence can be obtained locally.

There is also fishing in the Witcombe Reservoirs.

In addition there is to be taken into account the fishing in various Cotswold streams.

**Art Gallery.**—In Clarence Street (*see* p. 54).

**Banks.**—All the principal banks have branches in town.

**Baths.**—*Open-air pool* at south end of Sandford Park Recreation Ground, Keynsham Road, with café, sunbathing terrace and car park.

*Pittville Swimming Pools* adjoining Pittville Gardens, and opened in 1971, has a main $33\frac{1}{3}$ metre pool suitable for national events and international water polo.

*Montpellier Baths*, Bath Road. Wash baths.

**Bowls.**—The greens of the Cheltenham Bowling Club are in Suffolk Square.

Cheltenham Spa Bowling Club has greens in St. George's Square, at the west end of the High Street.

Whaddon Bowing Club has greens in Whaddon Road.

CHELTENHAM

## Churches and Chapels.—

CHURCH OF ENGLAND.—*St. Mary's* (Parish Church), off High Street; *St. Matthew's*, Clarence Street; *Christ Church*, Malvern Road; *St. James's*, Suffolk Square; *Holy Apostles*, London Road; *Emmanuel*, Ewlyn Road; and numerous others.

BAPTIST.—*Salem*, Clarence Parade; *Cambray*, Cambray Place; *Charlton Kings*, Church Street; *Zion*, Pilley Lane.

UNITED REFORM.—*Highbury*, Oxford Street; *Union*, Deep Street, Prestbury; *St. Andrew's*, Fauconberg Road.

METHODIST.—St. George's Street; Great Norwood Street; Gloucester Road; Mersey Road, Whaddon.

FRIENDS.—Portland Street.

ROMAN CATHOLIC.—*St. Gregory's*, St. James's Square; *Sacred Heart*, Moorend Road, Charlton Kings; *St. Thomas More's*, Princess Elizabeth Way.

FIRST CHURCH OF CHRIST, SCIENTIST, Bayshill Road.

SPIRITUALIST.—Bennington Street.

JEWS.—St. James's Square.

SALVATION ARMY.—Bath Road and Tewkesbury Road.

PLYMOUTH BRETHREN.—Regent Street.

**Clubs.**—*New*, Montpellier Parade; *Constitutional*, St. George's Road; *Union*, Cambray Place; *Conservative*, Vittoria Walk; *Labour*, Royal Crescent; *Liberal*, Albion House, North Place; and many others.

**Cricket.**—Cheltenham Cricket Club, Victoria Ground, Prince's Street. County matches are played here during the Cricket Festival, in August, on the College Ground, Bath Road.

**Croquet.**—Cheltenham Croquet Club, Old Bath Road.

## Distances (by road).—

| | Miles | | Miles |
|---|---|---|---|
| Andoversford | 6 | Oxford | 42 |
| Bath | 43 | Painswick | 10 |
| Birmingham | 45 | Salisbury | 70 |
| Bristol | 43 | Stow-on-the-Wold | 18 |
| Broadway | 16 | Stratford-on-Avon | 31 |
| Burford | 23 | Stroud | 14 |
| Chipping Norton | 27 | Swindon | 32 |
| Cirencester | 16 | Tewkesbury | 9 |
| Evesham | 16 | Warwick | 38 |
| Gloucester | 9 | Winchcombe | 7 |
| London (rail 121¼ m.) | 98 | Witney | 30 |
| Northleach | 13 | Worcester | 25 |

**Early Closing.**—With some exceptions shops close early on Wednesdays.

**Entertainments.**—Plays, etc., at the Everyman Theatre in Regent Street, and at The Playhouse in Bath Road. At the latter on alternate weeks plays are staged by well-known Amateur Societies. There are three cinemas in the town.

During the summer bands play in the Imperial Gardens or the Town Hall. Some of the world's greatest artistes appear at the concerts in the Town Hall, and each May a competitive Musical

50

Festival is held which ranks high in importance among such British Festivals. The Cheltenham Festival (of British contemporary music) is held each year during the first fortnight in July. The Festival of Literature with talks by well-known personalities is held annually during the autumn. The Town Hall is also a popular place for dancing: with evening dances and balls which rank as social occasions of importance.

**Football.**—Rugby at the Athletic Ground; Association (Southern League) at Whaddon Road.

**Golf.**—On Cleeve Hill, and easily reached by bus, is the course of the *Cotswold Hills Golf Club.*

Two miles westward, at Charlton Kings, is the course of the *Lilley Brook Golf Club.*

18-hole approach course at Pittville.

**Hospitals.**—General Hospital, Sandford Road; Children's Hospital, Harp Hill; St. Paul's Hospital, Swindon Road; Delancey Hospital, Charlton Lane.

**Hotels.**—*See* pp. 10–12.

**Hunting.**—No fewer than nine packs meet within easy reach of Cheltenham, including the Cotswold and the North Cotswold, the Duke of Beaufort's, Lord Fitzhardinge's, Vale of White Horse, Heythrop, Croome and the Arle Court Harriers.

**Information Bureau.**—Municipal Offices, The Promenade.

**Library.**—Central Public Library in Clarence Street (*see* p. 53).

**Licensing Hours.**—10.30–2.30, 6–10.30; 6–11 Fridays and Saturdays; Sundays, 12–2, 7–10.30.

**Museum.**—In Clarence Street (*see* p. 53).

**Population.**—75,910.

**Parking Places.**—The principal places are in Promenade Gardens, adjoining the Promenade; the Municipal Car Park in Rodney Road (opposite the Town Hall); Cambray Place and Montpellier Walk. Disc parking zone in Town centre.

**Races.**—Course adjoins the Evesham road, to the north of the town. Meetings include such races as the National Hunt Festival, Cheltenham Gold Cup, etc.

**Tennis.**—Hard and grass public courts at Montpellier and Pittville. The most important private grounds are those of the East Gloucestershire Club in Old Bath Road.


Cheltenham is essentially a town of trees and open spaces, of elegant Regency buildings and imposing modern ones. Though its development was based on the medieval virtues of its natural springs, Cheltenham is now noted principally as a delectable residential and educational town, a festival centre for the Arts, a principal shopping centre and a holiday resort from which to explore the Cotswolds.

It has unusual advantages as a venue for conferences.

## The Town

At the beginning of the eighteenth century, Cheltenham was only a small township, straggling along a High Street which ran roughly east and west, with the Parish Church on its south side, and a Grammar School—founded in 1578 but now removed— on the north side.

This same High Street is a good place from which to start a walk round the town; though now it is busy with traffic and lined with modern shops. The *Plough*, one of the old coaching inns, is now a modern hotel.

Running southward from the High Street is the famous **Promenade**, spacious and with a double avenue of fine horse-chestnuts. On one side are luxurious shops, and on the other an attractive Regency terrace which now houses the Municipal Offices. These terraced houses, with their pleasing architectural lines and delicate ironwork balconies, are typical of the older private dwellings in all parts of the town.

At the Municipal Offices is the town **Information Bureau** where full particulars of accommodation and of the town's entertainment and sporting activities may be obtained.

Among lawns and flower-beds in the Gardens which front the Municipal Offices are the War Memorial, a bronze statue of Dr. Edward Adrian Wilson, a Cheltonian, who perished with Captain Scott in the Antarctic in 1912 (the statue, by the way, was modelled by Lady Scott) and the Neptune Fountain, shaded by weeping willows grown from that over Napoleon's tomb in St. Helena.

A hundred yards east of the Promenade is—

## The Town Hall

a handsome Renaissance building which is the centre of many of the town's social and cultural activities. The main apartment

52

is a fine hall used for
concerts, theatrical pro-
ductions, etc., and which
has an excellent dance
floor. The hall is the
scene of a number of
balls which are import-
ant social functions.
Famous artistes perform
at the frequent concerts
here, and on Sunday

evenings there are concerts which are extremely popular with
young people.

Also in the Town Hall is the **Central Spa and Lounge,** where
one may sip the Cheltenham waters in ease and comfort. (For a
note on the Waters, *see* p. 60.)

Adjoining the Town Hall are the terraced **Imperial Gardens.**
The old Winter Garden building was demolished during the war.
On the west side of the Promenade, opposite Imperial Gardens,
is another Georgian terrace, behind which stands the **Cheltenham
Ladies' College** (p. 58).

The Promenade ends just above the Imperial Gardens, but it is
worth continuing further south, beyond the *Queen's Hotel*, to the
**Montpellier Gardens,** typical of the many pleasant little parks
which characterize Cheltenham. Here are a number of public
tennis courts and a putting course. Across the road is the **Rotunda,**
with its domed roof. Built originally as a Pump Room, it is now
occupied by Lloyds Bank. The adjoining row of shops in Montpellier Walk is interesting for the way in which the fronts are
upheld by a series of caryatides—willing slaves who regard with
complacency the parked cars of customers, far cry as it is from
flowing Greek garments to petrol.

Returning almost to the High Street, and turning to the left,
one comes to Clarence Street, in which is housed—

### The Library, Art Gallery and Museum

The Lending Library contains some 90,000 volumes, and in the
Reference Library on the left is a well-arranged collection of

41,000 books. There is also a Record Library and a Children's Library.

Branch libraries are situated at Hesters Way and Hatherley, the latter supplemented by a mobile library.

The entrance to the **Art Gallery and Museum** is at the east end of the building. Here again one encounters a collection that is both well chosen and well arranged. The gallery originated in a collection of pictures presented by the late Baron de Ferrieres and including works by such famous Dutch artists as Teniers, Metsu, Gerard Dou; and since then it has been augmented by paintings by a number of well-known British artists. About sixteen temporary exhibitions are displayed annually.

The **Museum** contains a good geological collection, and a large number of local birds and animals and objects associated with the archaeology of the district. In this connection special interest attaches to the exhibits relating to the Cotswold Wool industry. There is also a good display of glass, ceramics and Cotswold crafts and furniture. The Chinese Porcelain Room houses choice examples of oriental art. A Georgian Room and a Victorian Kitchen are also on view.

Near by is—

## The Parish Church

whose spire is prominent in many distant views, but the building itself is so tucked away behind shops and houses that many strangers to the town have difficulty in locating it. The church lies in the angle formed by Clarence Street and High Street, just west of the traffic roundabout, and is reached by passages between various buildings.

The church, a cruciform building, is spacious and dignified and has a notable number of stained-glass windows. The north transept has an excellent rose window in its east wall. The old north porch is now the Baptistery: note the nicely vaulted roof. On the north wall of the chancel are ancient brasses commemorating Sir William Grevill and his wife, and in the south-east corner is a graceful pillar piscina.

Many visitors consider that the memorials are not the least interesting feature of Cheltenham Church. In the north-west angle of the tower arches, for example, note the inscription to Hannah Forty, who for over 43 years was "a pumper at the Old Well". The Skillicorne memorial nearer the pulpit is worth reading. In the north transept is a tablet commemorating a death from "poison administered by the hands of a cruelly wicked livery servant"—by contrast note near the south door "The sad memorial of John English . . . to Jane his most deare wife."

54

Cheltenham, of course, has a more than local fame for curious epitaphs. In the churchyard, beside the path at the north-east corner of the church, and near the tall preaching cross, is a flat stone inscribed:

> Here lies John Higgs,
> A famous man for killing pigs;
> For killing pigs was his delight
> Both morning, afternoon and night.
> Both heats and cold he did endure,
> Which no physician could ere cure;
> His knife is laid, his work is done,
> I hope to heaven his soul is gone.

Close by is an inscription, of which variations are found in various parts of the country, to a deceased blacksmith:

> My Sledge and Hammer lies declined,
> My Bellows pipe have lost its Wind,
> My Forge is extinct, my Fire's decay'd
> And in the dust my Vice is layed.
> My Coal is spent, my Iron's gone,
> My Nails are drove, my Work is done.

The celebrated epitaph which follows is unfortunately spurious:

> Here lie I and my two daughters,
> Who died through drinking Cheltenham waters.
> If we'd stuck to Epsom salts
> We shouldn't be lying in these damp vaults.

To the south of the Parish Church a hundred yards away is **St. Matthew's Church**, a modern chapel of ease. Over the south porch is a good carved group, but the most notable feature of the building is the effect of vastness in the interior produced by the absence of pillars and the smallness of the sanctuary.

In this connection it is interesting to compare St. Matthew's Church with the **Roman Catholic Church of St. Gregory**, a short distance westward and recognizable for its fine steeple with clock.

To the north of the High Street, almost opposite the Promenade, is the reconstructed **Pittville Street**, leading in little over half a mile to Evesham Road running between **Pittville Park** and **Pittville Gardens**.

**Pittville Park**, eighteen acres in extent, lies to the west of the Evesham Road. It may be entered from the road itself or by means of a subway from the Gardens across the way. The principal feature of the gardens is the lake, shaded by lovely trees and graced by swans and various wild fowl. Boats can be hired and around the lake are numerous seats where one may rest and admire the charming scene.

**Pittville Gardens,** to the east of the road, are laid out in a more formal manner than the Park, with lawns, flower-beds, lake and rock gardens. At the far end is the beautiful—

## Pittville Pump Room

The Pump Room was built by Mr. Joseph Pitt, M.P., who in 1825 bought the Pittville estate and laid out the gardens.

The Ionic Colonnade around three sides of the Pump Room is a copy of that of the temple on the Ilissus at Athens. The Pittville building, however, has a beauty denied to that of its Greek predecessor, for it is built of Cotswold stone which the years have tinted to a very lovely shade of brown: a tint which no marble of Greece could ever attain. Above the colonnade a broad terrace has been opened where a glorious view southward is obtained.

The magnificent rooms on the top floor are used by the Gloucestershire College of Art for their Architectural School. The ground floor assembly hall and adjoining rooms are in constant use for presentation of social attractions, conferences and banquets. The Pump Room is a beautiful building and well worth inspection. In recent years a great deal has been spent on renovation and for provision of bar and catering facilities.

Cheltenham is liberally provided with parks and open spaces, and one of the delights of a walk through its shady thoroughfares

56

is the probability of coming across a playing field connected with one of the colleges or schools. In addition to Pittville Park and Gardens and Montpellier Gardens, which have already been mentioned, **Sandford Park** has become a very popular rendezvous. It lies between Bath Road and College Road and can also be entered from the High Street. The feature of the park is the trees and flower-girdled lawns and the water garden in which the river Chelt is induced to play a very attractive role. That part of Sandford Park east of College Road is laid out as a Recreation Ground, on the south side of which is a modern open-air **Swimming Pool** (*see* p. 49).

The acreage at Cheltenham devoted to open floral spaces, to recreation grounds and parks, is probably exceptional among towns of its size. Even the roundabouts which aid traffic are converted into delightful flower-beds, breaking up carefully-kept grass surfaces.

As an educational centre, Cheltenham is of high standing. In addition to Cheltenham College, the Ladies' College, the Grammar School, and various other schools for boys and girls, there is a fine Technical College, and two training Colleges for teachers. The future possibility of a University is already spoken of.

## Cheltenham College

In 1840 a few parents whose sons were being educated at private schools in Cheltenham decided to found a new school in accordance with their own principles. The first intention was to build in the central part of Cheltenham, but it soon became evident that considerable space would be required and the present site on the Bath Road was selected. This formed part of the grounds of Thirlestaine House, a magnificent building which was acquired by the College in 1948. The College buildings stand in grounds of 85 acres.

The first of the Cheltenham buildings, known as "The Big Classical", was completed within a year to the design of a Bath architect, James Wilson. The Old Chapel, built in 1858, has been replaced by the fine new Chapel added later to commemorate the Jubilee of the School. This is a very notable Perpendicular building, with a stone vaulted roof. A Cloister was added as a memorial to old Cheltonians who fell in the 1914–18 War.

To commemorate the Centenary of the College, a new block of modern classrooms was added; each room being named after one of the first thirteen Old Cheltonian winners of the Victoria Cross.

The College owns a Park, known as Reeves Field (after its donor), and extensive playing fields. On one the Cheltenham County Cricket Festival is held.

Close to the main building are the Boarding Houses, Swimming Bath, Engineering Workshop and Drawing Office, and squash, fives and tennis courts, and there is a boat-house at Tewkesbury.

The College comprises a Senior and Junior School. In the former the boys follow a general course of work up to the G.C.E. Advanced Level, or the University or Services Entrance Examinations.

Of the many famous Old Cheltonians mention might be made of Dr. Adrian Wilson of Antarctic fame, after whom the Biological Laboratories are named, and Field-Marshal Sir John Dill, one of the architects of victory in the Second World War.

To the west of the Promenade, between Montpellier Street and Bayshill Road, is the imposing, though not architecturally notable, group of buildings comprising—

### Cheltenham Ladies' College

Officially the founders of Cheltenham Ladies' College were the six men who, in 1853, drew up a prospectus for "A College for the education of young ladies and children under eight," and who in the next year opened school at Cambray House. Actually, however, the founder of the College as it stands today was Miss Dorothea Beale, who came in 1858, at a time when affairs were in a somewhat critical state. For just on fifty years, until her death in 1906, this remarkable woman ruled Cheltenham Ladies' College and the wisdom and foresight of her rule did much to develop the higher education of women.

There are 700 boarders, divided amongst twelve Houses, and about 100 day girls. The College is divided into Upper and Lower College. From the age of eleven-plus the girls have an all-round education and many go on to university or medical school. They can also specialize in music or art.

Needless to say, recreation and sport take proper place in the life of the College, which has several large playing fields, and also a swimming bath.

## Other Educational Establishments

The **Boys' Grammar School** was rebuilt in 1887–9 on the site of the original school in the High Street founded by Richard Pate in 1578. A new school is in Princess Elizabeth Way. The **Girls' Grammar School** is in Albert Road, near the Pittville Pump Room.

**Dean Close School** for boys was founded in 1886 in the western outskirts of the town, at Shelburne Road. **St. Paul's and St. Mary's Colleges** are Church Training Colleges for men and women teachers.

In Albert Road is the **Gloucestershire College of Art,** and the **North Gloucestershire College of Technology** lies to the south of the town.

## The Cheltenham Waters

The exploitation of Cheltenham's natural waters is said to have started with the observation in 1716 that pigeons liked the grains of salt which formed on the ground near a spring. This explains the prominence of pigeons on the town's coat of arms and crest.

Mineral water springs are found in many parts of the town but the only one available for public use is the Pittville Water which is available at the Town Hall Central Spa. The Pittville Water is the only natural alkaline water in this country.

## Cheltenham's History

Standing at the point where the principal road through the Cotswolds crosses that running along the western edge of the range, the site of Cheltenham was probably occupied from very early days, but the Cheltenham we know is mainly a creation of the past 200 years, originating in the discovery of the healing waters and taking a fresh impetus from the realization that its air was suitable for the retirement of those accustomed to warmer climates than that of England—an impetus which was strengthened by the establishment of the college for boys and, later, the Ladies' College.

It was in 1738 that the first spa was built by that versatile seaman, Captain Skillicorne, who is so fulsomely commemorated in St. Mary's Church. The development of the waters was continued by his son, William, and then Henry Thompson built the Montpellier Pump Room, to which were added the Rotunda and the Montpellier Gardens. About this time Joseph Pitt, M.P., bought and developed the Pittville estate, and the Promenade originated in a short-lived spa on the site of the *Queen's Hotel*. Other wells were opened and converted into Spas, but today the waters are available only from the Central Spa in the Town Hall.

All this time Cheltenham had been increasingly the resort of people of wealth and fashion, but the event which set the seal upon the success of the Spa was the visit of George III in 1788. He was accompanied by the Queen, the Princess Royal and the Princesses Augusta and Elizabeth, and formality was to be dispensed with, for the King had been advised by his physician to come and take the Cheltenham waters. Accordingly at 6 a.m. each morning His Majesty attended the Spa and in between glasses took the walking exercise which was the prescribed accompaniment to that refreshment, and during the rest of the days he walked and rode about and around the town with none of the ceremonial which encompasses reigning monarchs. For the best account of the various amusing events of that memorable visit it is necessary to turn to the *Diary* of Fanny Burney: a briefer series of vignettes is to be found in *At Cheltenham*, in which Miss Humphris and Captain Willoughby entertainingly describe the Georgian age in this most Georgian town.

Needless to say, the visit of the Royal family brought large and fashionable crowds to Cheltenham. An Assembly Room was opened in 1816 by no less a figure than the Duke of Wellington, and the King so much enjoyed his visits to the Theatre (where the Siddons and Kemble family had performed years before) that he created it a Theatre Royal. The roll of artists, writers and musicians who have stayed at or resided in Cheltenham is too long to be recited here, but it includes such names as Sir Walter Scott, Byron, Tennyson (part of *In Memoriam* was written at Cheltenham), Adam Lindsay Gordon (whose father was a master at the College), James Elroy Flecker (whose father was Head Master at Dean Close School). Three notable women writers must be mentioned: Mrs. Craik, D. K. Broster, and Margaret Kennedy, and other names taken almost at random from the list include Dr. Jenner, the inventor of vaccination (wall plaque in Alpha House, St. George's Road); such musicians as Gustav Holst and John Barnett, and artists such as Briton Rivière. All these people have left their impress upon Cheltenham; indefinably, perhaps, but the impression is there, together with half a hundred other and highly varying impressions, so that as the warm brown stone of the houses seems to ripen with the years, so the social atmosphere of the town takes on an added tinge of dignity with the memory of the many gay and witty and wise men and women who have lingered in the Promenade or looked down on the town from the neighbouring hills.

# Ward Lock's
# Red Guides

Edited by Reginald J. W. Hammond

**Complete England**

**Complete Scotland**

**Complete Wales**

**Complete Ireland**

**Lake District** (*Baddeley*)

**Complete Devon**

**Complete South-East Coast**

**Complete Yorkshire**

**Complete Scottish Lowlands**

**Complete Cotswolds and
  Shakespeare Country**

**Complete Thames and Chilterns**

**Complete Wiltshire and Dorset**

**Complete Cornwall**

**WARD LOCK LIMITED**

# Excursions from Cheltenham

In addition to the local bus and coach services, coach tours are operated by **Black and White Coaches Limited** from Cheltenham Spa to all surrounding beauty spots, including the Cotswolds, the Wye Valley, Forest of Dean, Malvern Hills and Shakespeare Country.

Cheltenham is so well placed for visiting all parts of the Cotswolds that no special directions are necessary and it will be sufficient to refer readers to the Index at the end of this Guide. Two hill-excursions there are, however, which may be regarded as Cheltenham's own: that to Leckhampton and Birdlip and that to Cleeve Common.

## Leckhampton Hill and Birdlip

This excursion affords the very finest series of views near the town and indeed for a considerable area around, and as it is on Cheltenham's doorstep (or should one say its rooftops?) it is open to all. Even those unable to walk any appreciable distance can travel by bus to the top of the hill, resting there while enjoying the view and then either returning by bus or gently walking back. The view on the right as one reaches the top of the hill is of wonderful extent and interest, while through the gardens on the other side are glimpses of the Devil's Chimney.

More active folk walk up the Bath Road past Cheltenham College, taking the left-hand fork at the *Norwood Arms*. As one ascends, Leckhampton quarries appear ahead, with the detached rock known as the **Devil's Chimney** to the right. Soon the road bears right along the face of the hill, and we may turn off on the left by Daisy Bank Road and soon find the obvious if somewhat steep way to the top. Another way is to keep to the main road as far as the lane leading to Salterley Grange Sanatorium. Follow this lane for about a hundred yards and then turn up on the left by the obvious path.

Those who come only as far as this, however, by no means exhaust the beauties or thrills of the excursion. Hardly more than a mile farther, for instance, after descending through woods and passing the *Air Balloon*, the view opens out again in even greater scope, including Gloucester and a great stretch of the Severn plain, through which the river itself makes a sinuous way, and beyond it the Forest of Dean and the mountains of mid-Wales. Below the road the ground is broken into little humps, making admirable places for a picnic.

On reaching **Birdlip** turn to the right, and then, opposite the *Royal George*, to the left, avoiding the steep descent of Birdlip Hill and entering **Buckholt Woods**. These lovely woods border our road for several miles, with glimpses through to the villages below and the reservoirs at Witcombe. The main Cheltenham–Stroud road is reached opposite Prinknash, and here we turn sharp to the right.

**Prinknash**, of old the property of the Benedictine Abbot of Gloucester, is interesting as now having a Benedictine Abbot of its own, for here have settled those Benedictine monks who for many years lived on Caldey Island, off the South Wales coast. In 1939 Dr. Hinsley, Cardinal Archbishop of Westminster, laid the foundation-stone of the new Abbey which the monks are building. The rebuilding of Prinknash Abbey was interrupted by the Second World War, but good progress is now being made.

From this point the road gradually runs down the western side of the hills, with grand·views over Gloucester (the Cathedral standing out well) to **Shurdington**. Beyond this point the road is an anticlimax, however, and it is preferable to turn off on the right by the lane which passes **Leckhampton Church**, with its lofty spire. Originally Norman, but enlarged in the fourteenth century and again in 1866, the church has little Norman work to show: though the font bowl is Norman. An unusual feature is the large sculptured head over the chancel arch: this was probably a ceiling boss in the tower and was removed when the bells were hung. The eastern end of the church is interesting for the way the chancel vaulting carries on the effect of the tower.

In the north-west corner is the tomb of Sir J. Giffard (d. 1330) and his wife, and in the south-west corner the effigy of a priest. The Giffards for centuries lived at **Leckhampton Court**, originally a fourteenth-century house; it was largely reconstructed in the

**Burford** (*A. Kersting*)

**Northleach** (*Eagle*)

**Fairford** (*Eagle*)

**Stanton** (*Eagle*)

nineteenth century, but retained the lovely old banqueting hall.

From the churchyard, Leckhampton Hill, a delightful viewpoint and a public pleasure ground, looks almost mountainous: those who wish to test their climbing powers can follow a footpath running eastward which will lead them to the Birdlip road.

## Cleeve Hill

The second excursion is that to **Cleeve Hill,** the highest point in the Cotswolds (over 1,000 feet above sea-level) and unsurpassed as a viewpoint. There are various routes from Cheltenham, the simplest being along the bus route through **Prestbury** and **Southam** (p. 68), though walkers will probably prefer the slightly longer but much less frequented ways starting by Charlton Kings and Battledown. There are some extremely fine approaches from the eastern side, notably that from Brockhampton and by White Hall Farm, and that from Winchcombe which includes Belas Knap (*see* p. 74).

Cleeve Hill is not merely high: it is an extraordinarily good viewpoint. As one climbs the road from Prestbury past hotels and tea gardens and cafés mile after mile of the plain opens on the left, with Gloucester, Tewkesbury, the Malvern Hills, the Forest of Dean, the Black Mountains—ridge after ridge in endless array, and at one's feet are villages like Bishop's Cleeve, Swindon, Stoke Orchard, many of which repay special visits (*see* pp. 67–69).

On Cleeve are the links of the **Cotswold Hills Golf Club** and here too, near that part of the Common known as Cleeve Cloud, is a **British Camp** which has been scheduled as an Ancient Monument.

**Huddlestone's Table,** below the Camp, is a great rough-hewn slab of rock traditionally said to mark the spot where Kenulf, King of Mercia, bade farewell to his royal and other guests who had come to Winchcombe for the dedication of the Abbey which he had founded and which was to have such a tragic connection with his son Kenelm (*see* p. 72). As an antiquity, however, neither the Camp nor the Table can compare with the wonderful long barrow of **Belas Knap,** some 2 miles east of this point (*see* p. 74). Walking across in this direction one appreciates the advantages of Cleeve as a view-point, for the views westward are matched in beauty, if not in extent, with those over to Winchcombe and the hills and woods beyond Charlton Abbots. For **Postlip** see p. 70. Visitors crowd along the western side of the Hill between the road and the precipitous drop to the plain below, but surprisingly few people appear to realize the beauties of this side of the Common.

### Elkstone and Coberley

This excursion introduces the visitor to some of the choicest and most varied scenery in the vicinity of Cheltenham. The first part is along the slope of Leckhampton Hills to **Birdlip,** as described on pp. 63–64. At Birdlip turn left, along the Roman *Ermine Street,* leaving it in a little over 2 miles by a left-hand turning leading to the village of **Elkstone** which in Domesday Book is referred to by its Saxon name *The Stone of Ealac.* The small stone preserved in the church vestry may be the tenth-century one from which the name of the village originated.

The church dates from 1160. The exterior is interesting for its fine tower with curious gargoyles, its scratch dials, votive crosses, carvings and the fourteenth-century south porch which

shelters an exceptionally good Norman doorway. One's admiration of the south doorway is mingled with surprise, first at finding Norman work at all and secondly at the richness and beauty of the moulding before us and of the tympanum with its sculpture of Christ Enthroned. Internally the effect of the Norman work is even finer, for beyond the splendid

66

Norman chancel arch is another, also richly chevroned, and in the east wall is a small but richly decorated Norman window. An unusual feature is the columbarium or dovecot above the chancel, reached by the newel stairway near the pulpit.

From Elkstone we descend rapidly to the Churn Valley near the fine park of **Cowley,** and then turn up the valley to **Coberley,** which with the **Seven Springs**—generally regarded as the source of the River Thames—is described on p. 134. Hence over Windlass Hill and down through Charlton Kings the return to Cheltenham is quite clear.


## BETWEEN CHELTENHAM AND TEWKESBURY

Nine miles of good road connect Cheltenham and Tewkesbury, but those who keep to the highway miss several scenes which are worth seeking out, and a far better plan if time allows is to make a haphazard way from village to village. Soon after leaving the outskirts of Cheltenham, for example, a turning on the right leads to—

### Swindon

—not by any manner of means to be confused with its bigger namesake in Wiltshire. The Gloucestershire Swindon is well known to archaeologists by reason of the tower of its church, which is very similar to that at Ozleworth (*see* p. 152), except for its position, which is at the west end of the church and not, as at Ozleworth, in the centre. It is unlike the ordinary run of church towers, and all kinds of speculations have been made as to its original function. One suggestion is that the present nave, erected over a century ago, occupies the site of what was the chancel, in which case the whole building may have been connected with the Templars. (It will be recalled that the Temple Church, in London, for example, consists of a round nave from which opens a chancel.) There are two-light windows at the top of each face of the hexagon, and on the northern side is a Norman doorway; but the window on the western face of the tower is a fourteenth-century insertion.

From Swindon, a pleasant cross-country road leads north-east crossing the main A435 road after one mile and in another mile we reach Southam.

## Southam

Southam, or Southam Delabere, is notable for a splendid tithe barn, of wood and stone, attached to *Pigeon House Farm*—a partly fourteenth-century building. Equally charming is the manor-house, the front dated 1631 but the half-timbered back of earlier date. In the face of this group of lovely buildings the little buttressed Norman chapel is rather disappointing, having been altered considerably during the last century to serve as Southam Church. The best features are the Renaissance stalls and a picture showing the legend of St. Veronica. From Southam, the road runs east for a quarter of a mile, then meets the main road to Winchcombe. Turn left here and continue a short distance to the fork where take the minor road on the left which leads to Bishop's Cleeve.

## Bishop's Cleeve

derives its name from its position at the very foot of the *cliff* culminating in Cleeve Common and the fact that it was once attached to Worcester. It has one of the finest churches in Gloucestershire—interesting both inside and out. The west front is distinguished by a pair of turrets which contain gallery stair-ways (one is supported by a wholly disproportionate buttress), and between these turrets is an exquisite Norman doorway, almost rivalled by that on the south by which we enter the church. Immediately attention is attracted by the wide Tudor arches of the arcade separating the nave from the north aisle, but the best features are the arches at the east end of the aisles and the splendid Jacobean oak gallery at the western end. Of the monuments, that to the Delaberes is outstanding, both for the effigies and for the admirably worked tomb.

Those interested in Cotswold tithe-barns will find at Bishop's Cleeve a good example which has recently been restored and converted for use as the village hall: it is opposite the former

68

Rectory, which was at one time a residence for the Bishop of Worcester. Much building has taken place here since the war, but the pleasing open lay-out of the housing estate has not spoiled the character of the village.

The road leads westward to **Stoke Orchard,** where there is an unspoilt small Norman church with Norman font, Elizabethan benches and a Jacobean pulpit. A late twelfth-century mural depicting the life of St. James stretches round the nave. And so to **Tredington,** where is another attractive unspoilt church. Here nave and aisles have not been added, and this enhances the appearance of the very low chancel arch, which dates from about 1150. The bench ends in the nave are nineteenth-century reproductions of the old seventeenth-century panels, though the seats and backs are mostly medieval. The chancel with its interesting stone bench against its north wall is probably the nave of the original church. If Tredington church had nothing else to show these features alone would be worth coming to see. But in addition is the splendid north doorway with its tympanum showing Christ in glory and the graceful old cross in the churchyard which completes a memorable picture. In the paving of the south porch is a fossilized ichthyosaurus—possibly the oldest thing in the county.

# The North-western Edge

## Cheltenham to Broadway and Chipping Campden

Although, since it provides a convenient arrangement, we describe the various places between Cheltenham and Broadway in the course of a single excursion, it must not be thought that this is the normal or indeed even a reasonably good way of visiting them. Nearly all these places lie among trees at the foot of the hills, all of them have roads or tracks running up into the hills, but hardly one of them is best appreciated unless one comes down to it from the hills. That is one of the reasons why so many journeys over the western side of the Northern Cotswolds develop into a series of divergences.

Beyond **Prestbury,** now practically part of Cheltenham, and conspicuous for its racecourse and polo ground, the road begins the long climb to **Cleeve Hill,** the views on the left gradually increasing in scope and spreading beyond Woodmancote and Bishop's Cleeve (*see* p. 68), now almost at our feet, far out into the Severn Plain. Cleeve Common has been described among the Cheltenham excursions.

**Postlip** is notable for its beautiful Elizabethan manor-house to which is attached an exquisite Norman chapel, long used as a barn but in recent times restored to its original purpose. The chapel is beautifully situated in the grounds of the house, and is approached between lawns by two flights of wide stone steps. The south door and the chancel arch are evidence of its Norman origin, but more interesting are the deeply-splayed Norman windows in the side walls and the opening, high up in the south wall of the nave, where used to shine the "Poor Souls' Light"— a lamp set up each evening to remind passers-by to pray for the souls of the departed.

Postlip is all too often overlooked by hurrying travellers, for it stands where the long ascent from Cheltenham has been succeeded by the long descent to Winchcombe, which is soon seen as a long streak of grey among the varied greens of trees and fields at the foot of the hills in front, the grey mass of Sudeley standing finely among trees to the right.

## Winchcombe

**Access.**—Bus and coach from Cheltenham, Gloucester, Broadway, etc.
**Banks.**—*Lloyds, Midland.*
**Hotels.**—*See* p. 12.
**Early Closing.**—Thursday.
**Folk Museum.**—Town Hall.
**Population.**—4,070.

Winchcombe is a fine example of a small Cotswold town fitting naturally into the surroundings. The houses, built of the local stone, nestle in a lovely well-wooded valley; from many points on the hills one can look down upon Winchcombe, and from all sides it is beautiful. Ancient houses, historic inns, a fine church are overlooked by a castle and neighboured by the ruins of Hayles Abbey and the prehistoric Belas Knap (*see* p. 74).

The history of Winchcombe extends back beyond the Conquest, to the days when it was the capital of Winchcombshire, and was surrounded by walls and gates, and the Abbot of Winchcombe sat in Parliament.

The origin of Winchcombe is bound up with the origin of its abbey, founded by Kenulf, King of Mercia, in the eighth century. It was burned by the Danes, rebuilt in the eleventh century, burned down again 200 years later and again rebuilt. In 1539 it

71

was dissolved, and its destruction was entrusted to Thomas Lord Seymour of Sudeley. Such is a brief outline of the history of this great group of buildings, but its brevity is nothing to the completeness with which the abbey has vanished. With difficulty can one visualize Winchcombe as the scene of the happenings related by William of Malmesbury in connection with the martyrdom of the boy Kenelm, who at the tender age of seven succeeded to the throne and around whose small body the great abbey increased in stately grandeur.

"Kenulf, King of the Mercians, his father, had consigned Kenelm, when seven years old, to his sister Quendrida, for the purpose of education. But she, falsely entertaining hopes of the kingdom for herself, gave her little brother in charge to a servant of her household with an order to dispatch him. Taking out the innocent under the pretence of hunting for his amusement or recreation, he murdered and hid him in a thicket. But strange to tell, the crime which had been so secretly committed in England gained publicity in Rome by God's agency, for a dove from heaven bore a parchment scroll to the altar of St. Peter containing an exact account both of his death and place of burial. . . . In consequence of a letter from the Pope to the Kings of England acquainting them with the martyrdom of their countryman the body of the innocent was taken up in presence of a numerous assembly and removed to Winchcombe. The murderous woman was so indignant at the chanting of the priests and the murmur of the people that she thrust out her head from the window of the chamber where she was standing and, by chance having in her hands a Psalter, she came in course of reading to the Psalm *Deus laudem meam* (Psalm 109), which, for I know not what charm, reading backwards she endeavoured to drown the joy of the choristers. At that moment her eyes were torn by divine vengeance from their hollow sockets."

Like that of Becket at Canterbury, the enshrined body of Kenelm was visited by thousands of pilgrims, bringing enormous importance and prosperity to Winchcombe. Weekly markets, horse and other fairs also attracted people and money to the town. During the sixteenth century, tobacco-growing flourished, but this source of revenue was much resented by the West Indian tobacco merchants and the industry dwindled away. Some of the lovely houses built in the prosperous years still stand near the church, around Abbey Terrace, and along Gloucester Street. Small picturesque cottages line the old drive to Sudeley, Vineyard Street: at the river in this same street is the spot of the old Ducking

Pond where husbands used to duck scolding wives and so-called witches. The street was originally called Duck Street. The Town Hall, although graced by the old stocks, is a nineteenth-century building. In one of the rooms is a small folk museum, open at certain times. The *George Inn* still preserves part of a medieval gallery used by the pilgrims to the abbey. An old pottery north of the village may be visited.

## Winchcombe Parish Church

The Parish Church, built in the fifteenth century, is a good example of the Perpendicular style. Its exterior is fascinating for its forty grotesque gargoyles, the battlemented tower and crocketed pinnacles. The interior is light and spacious; points of interest are the canopied niches, the font, candelabrum and an altar cloth embroidered by Katharine of Aragon. The south porch has fine fan vaulting.

## Sudeley Castle

*The Gardens and castle are open to visitors every afternoon from March to October. Fee.*

The original castle was built in the reign of Stephen and rebuilt by Ralph de Boteler in the fifteenth century. Part of this castle has survived and includes the chapel and the ruins of the fine banqueting hall. Sudeley has had many changes of ownership and has been the property of the Crown. Queen Elizabeth I, Anne Boleyn, Katharine Parr (who

73

is buried here), Charles I and other members of the Royal Family have lived or visited here. Miles Coverdale, translator of the Bible, was chaplain at the time of Katharine Parr.

The Castle is still occupied. It was bought by the *Dent* family who restored it for use as a private manor-house. It is a dignified Cotswold stone building in a beautiful setting, with terraces and lovely gardens surrounded by fine yew hedges. In the panelled library are fine pictures, tapestry and furniture, etc., of great historic interest and beauty.

## Belas Knap

This very important archaeological remain lies high on the hills between Winchcombe and Charlton Abbots, and since its situation is almost as fine as its construction the excursion is one which can be recommended to all who like a good walk.

At the south-western end of Winchcombe turn out of the Cheltenham road by that leading to Andoversford and shortly climbing steeply to the woods above Corndean. At the fork there is a choice of ways: the nearest approach by road is that to the right, the rather rough lane to Wontley Farm being followed upward until the way is barred by a gate beside a barn. Just beyond the gate an opening in the wall on the left indicates a path across the field to an opening in the opposite wall; beyond which bear half-right (crops permitting, of course) and there will be seen, just beyond the corner of the field, the grass-covered hump which is Belas Knap.

The alternative route from the fork mentioned above is by the Andoversford road for about a hundred yards or so, and then by a clear path which ascends through the woods to the right, entered by a swing gate. The route has been well signposted by the Ancient Monuments department.

**Belas Knap** is one of the finest existing examples of a Stone Age burial-mound. Poised on the hilltops nearly 1,000 feet above the sea, it dates from about 1400 B.C., and consists of a long whale-back mound surrounded by a ditch and differing from most other barrows of its age in having no central burial-chamber. When it was opened in 1863–4 thirty-eight skeletons were found. At the north-western end are two horn-like projections having between them what appears to be a doorway, which is in fact a dummy. In this connection H. J. Massingham is instructive (*Wold Without End*):

74

"That false portal . . . is a perfect illustration of that tyranny of custom which can be so heartbreaking in other walks of life. When the central chamber fell into disuse, the megalith builders still continued at prodigal labour erecting massive stone portals for no purpose whatever except that their fathers had done so before them . . ."

Belas Knap has been restored by the Department of the Environment, so that the beautiful dry-walling of which the horns are comprised is not necessarily all ancient work, but enough remains of the old structure to indicate the care and skill of those builders of nearly 4,000 years ago.

From Belas Knap one can return to Winchcombe by either of the routes outlined above, or one can follow the rough lane to Wontley Farm and there turn westward across Cleeve Common; eastward to Charlton Abbots or keep more or less straight ahead down into the valley and by White Hall Farm come to the road again near Brockhampton. Another way down to Charlton Abbots is to skirt the upper edge of the wood until, about half a mile south of Belas Knap, a track at the end of the wood leads down to the road near Goldwell Farm.

**Charlton Abbots** is a small hamlet lying just off the road and with a tiny church. It was once the property of Winchcombe Abbey and the local yard known as *Lepers' Yard* is a reminder that the monks installed a leper house here. The church was largely rebuilt in the nineteenth century but the lovely Elizabethan Manor-House has retained its gracious dignity.

Looking across the valley, the plantation near Sudeley Castle is **Spoonley Wood.** Here is the neglected site of a large Roman Villa which had a huge granary. Unfortunately the site has not been given official protection, and the few attempts which have been made to shelter the tessellated pavements from the weather are pitifully inadequate.

At neighbouring Wadfield Farm are extensive remains of a Roman Villa.

To the west of Winchcombe **Langley Hill** rises to over 900 feet above the sea. It is worth climbing for the fine views from the camp-crowned summit—to the one side Winchcombe among the wooded hills of the western edge; to the other, Oxenton Hill and **Bredon Hill** and the great Severn Valley, with the Malverns to the north-west and away in the south-west the Forest of Dean hills.

Ensconced on the northern side of Langley Hill is **Stanley Pontlarge**, taking its name not (directly, at any rate) from a bridge, but from Robert de Pont l'Arch, who owned it in the fourteenth century. It is a tiny farming hamlet with a tiny church worth visiting for its Norman doorway, window and chancel arch, the piers of the latter now much out of the perpendicular.

## Winchcombe to Hayles Abbey

Hayles (or Hailes) Abbey, about 3 miles to the north-east of Winchcombe, attracted pilgrims in the Middle Ages to view the "Relic of the Holy Blood". Pilgrims also visited the shrine of Kenelm at Winchcombe and in these days Hayles offers us what Winchcombe cannot—the sight of some remains of its once beautiful abbey.

The most direct path is by the *Pilgrims' Way* leaving the main road immediately beyond the point where it crosses the river at the northern end of Winchcombe; motorists and cyclists must keep to this road for about 3 miles, to where a signpost on the right points the way. For those with time, however, a much more attractive route is to ascend the hill past Sudeley Castle and through the woods, forking to the left near the top along the Ford road and in about half a mile taking a lane on the left. The lane is part of the Saltway and descends steeply to the village of Hayles, where bear round to the right for the Church and the remains of the Abbey.

Yet another route, even more pleasant, is to keep along the Ford road for a mile or so further, then turning off on the left for the aptly-named hamlet of **Farmcote**, where stands a seldom-used but well-cared-for small church, once the nave of the chapel of ease. Its interest is in the Norman belfry, arches and font, and the seventeenth-century pulpit and sanctuary rails.

Two beliefs associated with Farmcote may be mentioned. One is to the effect that an underground passage connected it with Hayles; the other that the seat overlooking Hayles from *Beckbury Camp* marks the spot whence Thomas Cromwell watched the destruction of the Abbey.

Beyond Farmcote the road becomes a rough track dipping through the woods and opening up lovely views of the scene below: at all seasons this is the best approach to Hayles.

## Hayles Abbey

Admission.—*Charge* to Abbey and Museum. Open standard hours, Sundays from 2 p.m.

When in danger of shipwreck off the Scilly Isles, Richard, Earl of Cornwall, a brother of Henry III, vowed that if he landed safely he would build an abbey for the white monks of Citeaux in the same way that John, his father, had built Beaulieu, where Richard's wife had recently been buried. The work was pressed forward with such speed that the abbey was completed in the short space of eight years (1245–53), the dedication ceremony taking place in 1251 in the presence of Henry III and the Queen, thirteen bishops, five abbots, and 300 knights. In 1270 the importance of the abbey was immensely increased by the second Earl of Cornwall's present of a phial supposed to contain some of the Holy Blood and vouched for by the Patriarch of Jerusalem and Pope Urban IV. A magnificent shrine was built to hold the precious relic, which at certain times was shown to the pilgrims who flocked to Hayles in their thousands, for such a treasure could be expected to hold powers of healing, and indeed Leland says, "God daily sheweth miracles through the virtues of the Precious Blood."

So for three centuries the fame and the fortunes of Hayles waxed strong; but then came a day when Latimer, Bishop of Worcester, demanded the surrender of the Abbey, and its contents and doom fell upon Hayles on Christmas Eve, 1539.

At that time the value of the Abbey was stated to be £330 2*s.* 2*d.* —a sum which would of course represent a much greater value than now. The place was stripped of its priceless jewels and decorations, and with the exception of the abbot's lodgings the main buildings were demolished, the leaden roofs being rolled up and carted off to the Tower of London for the King's use.

The end of the Relic is best described in the words of Latimer himself: "It was enclosed within a round beryl, garnished and bound on every side with silver, which we caused to be opened in the presence of a great multitude of people, being within a little glass; and also tried the same, according to our powers, wits and discretions, by all means and by force of the view and other trials thereof. We think, deem and judge the substance and matter of the supposed relic to be an unctuous gum coloured, which, being in the glass, appeared to be a glistering red, resembling partly the colour of blood; and after we did take out

77

part of the said substance and matter out of the glass, then it was apparent glistering yellow colour, like amber or base gold and doth cleave to, as gum or bird-lime."

With the exception of a few arches of the cloister walls, the abbey above-ground has vanished almost as completely as the precious Relic which brought it so much fame; but in 1936 the site was presented to the National Trust, who have cleared away the weeds and rubble and laid bare many of the foundations so that one can at least realize the extent of the buildings. The High Altar lay to the left of the path which passes the end of the Museum, and one can trace the outline of the five apsidal chapels built to form a corona and so increase the splendour with which the shrine became surrounded. The Department of the Environment are carrying out excavation work. An excellent little handbook can be obtained from the custodian.

**The Museum** is exceptionally well arranged and interesting, and should be seen by all who desire to conjure up a vision of the abbey as it was. There are life-size figures of Cistercian monks, there are various drawings of the ruins and some astonishingly fine and rare "Chertsey" tiles; large thirteenth-century bosses from the chapter-house roof and some equally fine bosses of the sixteenth century which belonged to the cloister, and a large assortment of carved stones indicating the great beauty of the buildings.

## Hayles Parish Church

across the road, was built in 1130 and therefore stood here before the Abbey. Later it probably became the Guest-House chapel, for it stands close to the site of the main entrance to the Abbey. Externally it is notable for its little half-timbered tower. "Inside it has features of almost every century. The open black and white timber roof is in good condition and the walls retain their plaster. The floor is stone-flagged where not lined with some 300 thirteenth-century heraldic tiles once brought from the Abbey. Upon the walls are remains of rare mural paintings attributed to Edward I's reign (c. 1300), incorporating armorial devices of Leon and Aragon, accompanied by De Valence and de Bryan. Furthermore, there is a magnificent Saint Cecilia depicted on a window jamb in the Chancel (1290). There is a mediæval oak rood-screen (untouched), a Jacobean pulpit and a box pew in the west end. Perhaps the most outstanding element in this unique and very small church is the Commonwealth arrangement in the chancel for the Puritanized Lord's Table. Although the seventeenth-century table now stands upon the original altar stone, the oak-panelled seats remain as the Puritan carpenter had so skilfully made and arranged them. . . ." (*W. St. Clair Baddeley.*)

A field-path from Hayles Church leads in rather more than a mile to **Didbrook,** worth visiting for its lovely old house and its church, which was rebuilt by Abbot Whitchurch of Hayles in the fifteenth century in consequence of having been the scene of the murder of some Lancastrian fugitives from Tewkesbury. Several unusual features will interest archaeologists: the treatment of the tower arches, for example (as contrasted with the wooden chancel arch) and the pieces of fifteenth-century glass in the east window asking prayers for the soul of Abbot Whitchurch, whose tomb lies in a canopied niche in the north wall of the nave. So to—

## Stanway

at the junction of two roads that climb the Cotswold escarpment, the straight and narrow "Old Hill" which was the ancient Stane Way and the "New Hill" which is the modern road—a road lovely with trees and lovely with views, especially at evening. Our road, however, crosses this highway and almost immediately brings us to the house which is the property of the Earl of Wemyss and March. The house is a delight, especially when seen from the north side of the churchyard. The impressive gatehouse bears the arms of John Tracy of Stanway and his wife Anne Atkyns. They married in 1701, some fifty years after the death of Inigo Jones to whom the gatehouse is often wrongly attributed. The

church has been so restored and altered as to retain little of general interest; always excepting the fact that in its graveyard lies Thomas Dover, the physician who discovered the use of quicksilver, or mercury, for medical purposes. Stanway, in fact, provides an interesting architectural object-lesson. On the one hand is the great manor-house with its grandiose gateway; on the other the church, which may once have had all the simple dignity of a Norman building but which now relies on other features for its appeal—and there, standing alone in the grounds of Stanway House, and beautifully set off by smooth lawns and trees which in early summer are a mass of blossom, is a building which is now lent for meetings and social events but which originated as a medieval tithe-barn of about 1400. Cotswold barns are outstanding, and this is one of the best, with a magnificent roof coming close down to the ground and carried by tremendous roof-trusses bedded low down into the walls. With its porch, buttresses and finials, it looks more like a church than a granary.

West of Stanway is **Toddington,** with a church "built at a cost of £44,000 by the 4th Lord Sudeley and designed by Mr. G. E. Street, architect of the Law Courts"; and a manor-house built about 1830 to replace a seventeenth-century mansion. Toddington has been the home of the Tracys from very early times, and it is more than probable that the old church supplanted by that of Mr. Street, architect of the Law Courts, was built in expiation of the murder of Thomas à Becket, for one of the knights concerned in that crime was Tracy of Toddington.

North of Stanway the road continues very happily to—

## Stanton

"many-gabled Stanton, drawn in under the ankles of the wolds", as H. J. Massingham puts it. Stanton has not a noticeably greater number of beautiful buildings than other Cotswold villages, but in the mysterious way that Cotswold villages have it contrives to display its charm in such a manner that it is frequently heralded as the most beautiful place in the district. Stanton, with its lovely old cross and its church spire hidden among the trees, must be entered very near the head of the list. The majority of the buildings are of Cotswold stone erected in the sixteenth and seventeenth centuries. They have been carefully

**The Paddock, Cheltenham Racecourse** (*Eagle*)

**Imperial Gardens and Queens Hotel, Cheltenham** (*Eagle*)

**Winchcombe** (*Eagle*)

**Broadway** (*Eagle*)

restored and kept in repair. On a sunny afternoon the effect of the grey-brown stone against a background of green—green of the village trees and of those on the hillside beyond—and great blazes of flowers of every hue is something that will linger in the memory; and in the face of such open-air beauty relatively few visitors will enter the church to see the vestiges of the Norman building which preceded the present Perpendicular structure, or to look for the curious panel, once in the roof but now in the south wall, commemorating one Mauriticus Wraybury, probably the donor of the aisle and roof. Stanton is fortunate in possessing a cricket pitch, and a bathing pool fed by natural springs.

Those who climb the hill behind the village by the track on the site of the seventeenth-century coach road, will, if they persevere, find themselves looking down across to **Snowshill** (described on p. 82), at the head of a combe running down to the plain and having on its threshold—

## Buckland

an attractive tree-shaded village typical of Cotswold in the unexpected richness and interest of its church. It is an Early

English building having in its east window some splendid fifteenth-century glass, which has been adjudged the finest in the Cotswolds, and which is thought to have come from Hayles Abbey at the Dissolution. It so impressed William Morris that he was instrumental in the releading of it. The window depicted the Seven Sacraments, though only three lights are now left entire, representing respectively Baptism, Marriage and Extreme Unction. The entrances to the rood-loft still remain, and the aumbry in the east wall of the nave shows that the loft had an altar. In the north aisle an inscription tells us "Thomas and James Sowthern of theyr own cherg have given this wainscot and benchin to the church in the yere of our Lord 1615". One of the treasures of Buckland is a fine piece of fifteenth-century embroidered needlework which was once an altar frontal; another is the ancient "Buckland Bowl", of maple wood and silver which has been in use at least since the sixteenth century, at one time as the village bridal bowl. Near the church, on the right lower down the hill, is the picturesque fifteenth-century Rectory, built by a former Rector, William Grafton, containing a fine hall of the period with fifteenth-century glass. Buckland is among the smallest of Cotswold villages and is a place of unusual charm.

In 2 miles the main road below the village would bring us to Broadway, but there is a more interesting way for walkers through Burhill woods and fields. The footpath is well defined and is about two and a half miles long.

## Snowshill

A good road now connects Broadway with Snowshill, an attractive village nestling in the folds of the hills 3 miles to the south. Tourists are attracted to this quiet little grey place mainly by **Snowshill Manor.** This lovely Tudor mansion with its terraced gardens is now in the care of the National Trust and is open to the public. (*May–September: Wednesday, Thursday, Saturday, Sunday and Bank Holidays. Weekends: April and October. Charge.*) It houses a varied collection of articles of historic interest—ancient clocks, toys, musical instruments and a selection of tools once used by spinners and weavers. The rest of the village clusters round a triangular green on which stands the nineteenth-century Parish Church.

## BROADWAY

Access.—By bus and coach from all neighbouring centres.
Banks.—*Lloyds, Midland.*
Distances.—Cheltenham, 15 miles; Evesham, 5½; Gloucester, 24; London, 92; Oxford, 36; Stow-on-the-Wold, 10; Stratford-on-Avon, 15; Winchcombe, 8.
Early Closing.—Thursday.
Golf.—18-hole course on Willersey Hill.
Hotels.—*See* p. 10.
Population.—2,503.
Post Office.—High Street.

It is the fashion among Cotswold-lovers to look askance at Broadway because of the crowds who pour into it every fine week-end and of the arrangements which have to be made to meet their needs. Such intolerant criticism, however, does the village a grave injustice. See it on a sunny morning before the crowds have begun to arrive, or at evening when the last coach has departed, and there is opportunity to make an unhindered and leisurely survey, and Broadway will rapidly disclose a charm which cannot be denied, whether one studies the effect of the broad way as it leads on to the steep ascent of Fish Hill or looks more closely at the many delightful houses which border it.

Broadway is far from being unadulterated Cotswold: even in the main street modern buildings obtrude and things have been done to old buildings which should never have been sanctioned; but taking all in all one can fairly say that while not every prospect pleases, most of them do (the new extensions along the Evesham road are not regarded as part of Broadway in this survey). Let us therefore regard Broadway as a pleasant place which has the misfortune to be popular, but which is nevertheless a place to be seen and to be enjoyed. The village might get along very well without the Cotswolds, but the time has not yet come when the Cotswolds can afford to disown Broadway. Walk from the *Lygon Arms* at the lower end of the Way to the house at the upper end so long the home of Madame de Navarro, who as Mary Anderson so graciously interpreted Shakespearian roles, and it will be conceded that Broadway is indeed very good to look upon, and if the modern parish church does not entirely please, persevere a little farther along the Snowshill road and you will come to **St. Eadburgha's Church.**

The building is as nearly in accord with the Cotswold spirit as any. Majestically it stands, at the edge of the meadows, cool and quiet; built of local stone and inside a harmony of warm, soft brown. No coloured glass clouds the windows, through which one looks out at the green of trees or, in winter, at tracery more delicate than was ever wrought in stone. The church is cruciform, the nave being divided

from the chancel by the tower, which is carried on singularly graceful arches. Adjoining the altar is an interesting palimpsest brass to Anthony Daston (1572) who "loved the world but now scorns its joys". This palimpsest brass formed part of a much larger (? Flemish) brass; another part is to be found at Westerham, Kent. Rubbings of the reverse sides of these Broadway and Westerham brasses are to be seen near the north door of the church. They show clearly that they were parts of the same original brass.

Also in the chancel is a fragment of carved panelling and in the south transept are fragments of old stone from various parts of the building. The tub-shaped font stands on a platform inlaid with old tiles. Such a catalogue of details does less than justice to a lovely old building and leaves much unnoticed—for instance, the timbers of the nave roof; but here as is often the case in the Cotswolds, the general effect is so beautiful that examination of individual components seems ungrateful. Here at any rate one can envision Broadway as it was before the days of petrol.

At the other end of Broadway the road climbs the hills in a series of wide zigzags which afford grand views over to the Malvern Hills and far beyond. From the *Lygon Arms* to the little *Fish Inn* it is a climb of some 600 feet, and even if one does not get all the way it is well worth walking at least part of the distance for the sake of the views. The finest prospects, of course, are from the top of **Broadway Beacon,** 1,024 feet above the sea and crowned by a **Tower** which, while it does not noticeably increase the range of the view from it, is a landmark for very many miles around. "At the end of the eighteenth century the ground on which it stands belonged to the Earl of Coventry, and the story goes [so Mr. H. A. Evans assures us] that the Countess wishing to see whether the spot could be seen from Croom Court, the family seat near Worcester, caused a bonfire to be lighted here. The fire being plainly visible, she persuaded the Earl to build a tower here." However satisfying the tower may have been to look at, the view from it is extraordi- narily fine, and one can picture the rapture with which William Morris, Ros- setti and Burne-Jones used to spend vacations here— rapture interrupted only by Rossetti's grumblings at having to carry food all the way up from Broad- way!

**The view** has been described time and again, and deservedly so, for not only in its extent is it so glorious but in the subtle and constant changes of colour. Its extent can best be expressed by remarking that the foreground is occupied by the Vale of Evesham, from which Bredon Hill rises like an island, far beyond which the long blue ridge of the Malverns and, farther south, the Forest of Dean lead the eye on to the Black Mountains of Wales. On a clear day one can pick out Eves- ham, Tewkesbury, and a score of villages; to the north and north- west the Lickey, Clent and Clee Hills may be seen and the Wrekin beyond. In spring the vale is a sea of fruit blossom, but whatever the conditions one feels that here one is at the threshold of another world. To come to Broadway Beacon, for example, from London, and to spend an hour or two in full view of this amazing panorama is to experience a feeling of escape, of a revitalized sense of proportion, as can normally be acquired only by a much longer stay in more distant places.

The charm of Broadway Beacon does not lie entirely in the distant view: away to the left the Wolds fall to the plain in a great cascade of wooded spurs and outliers, and whether one turns along the breast of this broken escarpment or over Middle

Hill, or follows the lane past the tower to where it is more recognizably **Buckle Street** (*see* p. 111) one will find scenes to remember.

Moreover, in gazing out into the Vale we are apt to overlook in more than one sense two villages tucked away at the very foot of the hills but a mile or so from Broadway and each very well worth visiting. The first is **Willersey**, "proper Cotswold. Bell Inn, duckpond, barn-church with its nice-square dump of a four-pinnacled tower and true old barn-houses are grouped around the green like casual knots of worthies delivering crop-gossip or weather-lore through the slow process of the years." Thus H. J. Massingham in that splendid book *Wold Without End*, whose summary of neighbouring **Saintbury** cannot be bettered: "Almost every house in Saintbury is separated from its neighbour by twists in the hillside or age-bent orchards or tipped-up pastures, and even the big chestnut in the centre is all to itself. The little steepled church, of Norman blood and Saxon lineage, likewise perches quite alone, not merely overlooking the vasty vale where Bredon and the Malverns stand like hippos in a shallow lake, but craning over it, a few steps and to topple into it, so abrupt is its cliff. Housen here and housen there, that is Saintbury."

Saintbury is indelibly associated with Algernon Gissing, one of that early band whose writings made Cotswold known to the outside world, and with one of its vicars—William Latimer, a translator of the New Testament.

An even greater name in Cotswold annals calls to us from the slopes above, however, for here is **Dover's Hill** (*see* p. 90) whereon for two centuries were held the great Olympick Games inaugurated by Robert Dover. But precedence must first be given to Chipping Campden, for the glories of Dover's Hill are entirely of the past, whereas Campden has come down to us from the past with its glories undimmed, and as its most famous son William Grevel was hailed as "The Flower of the wool merchants of all England" so is Campden the flower of the Cotswolds.

## CHIPPING CAMPDEN

**Access.**—By bus and coach from most neighbouring centres.
**Distances.**—Broadway, 5 miles; Cheltenham, 22; Evesham, 8; Moreton-in-Marsh, 7; Stow-on-the-Wold, 10; Stratford-on-Avon, 12.
**Early Closing.**—Thursday.
**Hotels.**—*See* pp. 10–12.
**Licensing Hours.**—10–2.30, 6–10.30; Fri. and Sat. till 11; Sundays, 12–2, 7–10.30.
**Population.**—1,956.

G. M. Trevelyan in his English Social History refers to Chipping Campden High Street as "the most beautiful village street in England". Few people would dispute this statement. The wide curving thoroughfare is an outstanding example of harmony in architecture. The mellowed Cotswold-stone houses, built more than six hundred years ago, combine gracefully with those built at various periods during the succeeding centuries. There are fourteenth-century houses and inns, a fifteenth-century grammar school building, seventeenth-century almshouses and market hall, and an eighteenth-century Town Hall.

Campden is the most typical of Cotswold towns, not merely in the pleasant dignity of its buildings, and in its air of quiet unobtrusive well-being, but in the notable absence of commercialism. Yet Chipping Campden *is* a show place, however little it may advertise the fact. The **Market Hall,** standing in an island in the centre of the main street, is a popular place from which visitors admire the view through the arches. This seventeenth-century building, now in the care of the National Trust, is part of the very marrow of Campden. The word Chipping is itself derived from the old word "ceapen" or market, and here for centuries was the meeting-place of those with wool to sell and those with money to buy it. For close on two hundred years Campden was a busy centre of the Cotswold wool trade. The

Normans began the wool-growing industry, and buyers came even from across the Channel to buy Cotswold wool. Then in the fourteenth century the trading centre was established at Calais, where wool was collected, taxed and sold, and though the Englishman's proverbial adaptiveness quickly showed him the most advantageous way of exporting his wool across the Channel the inevitable tendency was for the manufacture of woollen goods to be undertaken at home. Fortunately for the present appearance of the town, Campden was without the necessary water supply to enable it to set up weaving on a large scale, and the factories were built instead elsewhere. Since those days Campden has led a relatively sheltered life: quietly prosperous but with neither need nor desire to become industrial.

The most telling memorial of the greatness of the wool trade is Campden itself. Almost every house was obviously built by people of substance; note for example, almost opposite the end of Church Street, the beautiful building with its Gothic doorway and lovely bay windows and gables. This was built in 1380 by William Grevel, described on his fine brass inserted in the chancel floor of the Parish Church as "The Flower of the wool merchants of all England". Grevel lived in his house until he died in 1401, and contributed much to the beauty of Campden. He left large sums of money for restoration work and rebuilding of the parish church. Another benefactor was Sir Baptist Hicks, first Viscount Campden, who lived in the village at the beginning of the seventeenth century. He built the Market Hall and the almshouses and in 1613, a fine mansion south of the church. This house, surrounded

by lovely gardens and terraces was burnt down during the Civil War and all that now remains are the gateway (restored), two gatehouses and pavilions and the almonry. The almshouses, near by on a raised terrace, present a peaceful picture and have proved to be a more permanent testimony of Hicks's generosity. Beyond the almshouses rises the fine tower of—

## The Church

The former opulence of Chipping Campden is reflected in its church, which is a lofty and spacious building of altogether admirable proportions. These are particularly noticeable in view of the scarcity (in comparison, for example, with Burford) of monuments. In fact, the only obtrusive memorial in Campden Church is that in the chapel at the end of the south aisle commemorating Sir Baptist Hicks (*see* p. 88).

There are several fine brasses. The best of these commemorates William Grevel and his wife, with the proud tribute that he was the flower of all the wool merchants in England. Other brasses commemorate William Welley and his wife (1450) and William Gibbys and his wife and their thirteen children (1484). Note also the splendid fifteenth-century brass lectern and the carved pulpit, both presented by Sir Baptist Hicks. He also restored the fifteenth-century South Chapel in 1629 which serves as a family burying-place. There are some beautifully sculptured memorials to the Hicks family and it is usually referred to as *Hicks Chapel*.

The east window forms Campden War Memorial and is said to contain nearly 10,000 fragments of glass. Right at the top of the window are the only remaining pieces of the fifteenth-century glass with which the church was once adorned. An unusual feature of Campden Church

is the window over the chancel arch, like those at Northleach and Cirencester: it contributes not a little to the spacious appearance of the
interior.

The greatest treasures of Campden Church, however, are under the
tower. Here in large glass cases are some magnificent examples of
medieval embroidery, including fifteenth-century altar hangings and
a fine fourteenth-century cope. It is worth noting that by the special
desire of the late Queen Mary the altar frontal in Westminster Abbey
on the occasion of the coronation of George V was copied from these
beautiful embroideries.

## Dover's Hill

> "On Cotteswold hills there meets
> A greater troop of gallants than Rome's streets
> E'er saw in Pompey's triumph; beauties, too,
> More than Diana's beavie of nymphs could show
> On their great hunting days."

No account of Campden would be complete without some
reference to the Cotswold Games held on neighbouring Dover's
Hill. Their originator was Robert Dover, a retired attorney, "of
a generous, free and public spirit . . . nimble in all physical
exercise and most at home in the saddle. It is said that the games
were projected as a considered opposition to the Puritan sup-
pression of sport; however that may be, Dover made his plans,
selected the site and then approached Endymion Porter, a friend
at Court, who obtained not only the King's permission to hold
the games but 'some of the King's old cloaths, with a hat and
feather and ruff, purposely to grace him and consequently the
solemnity.' Porter, moreover, suggested the name 'Olympick' for
the games, whence later on Dover was hailed as 'The Great
Inventor and Champion of the English Olympicks, Pythicks,
Nemicks, Istmicks; the great Architect and Inginere of the
famous and admirable Portable Fabricke of Dover Castle, her
Ordnance and Artillery.' The Castle referred to was a portable
wooden affair with twin towers, each with a cannon. This was
placed upon the brow of Dover's Hill; from its staff a yellow
banner was unfurled; the cannon 'rattled to the skies', Dover
rode forth with all dignity in the King's old cloaths, a yellow
favour vying with the feather in his hat, and with a call upon
the bugle the Games began."

The nature of the programme varied from time to time during the two centuries the Games continued to flourish, but horse-racing always played a prominent part, as did coursing and cock-fighting, wrestling and dancing. As Ben Jonson put it—

> The Cotswold with the Olympic vies
> In manly games and goodly exercise,

and from all accounts "manly" was a modest description of the vigour with which the games were prosecuted. Probably not one visitor in a thousand has heard of the Cotswold shin-kickers, but that Cotswold encyclopaedia H. J. Massingham tells us in *Wold Without End*, "In the last century shin-kicking contests, village team against village team, were all the rage of North Cotswold. . . . At Yabberton I heard that an old warrior used to sit and have his shins beaten by a deal plank as a form of training while one of the heroes of Campden used to 'thrape' his shins with a hammer in order to be deemed worthy of inclusion in the team."

The Cotswold Olympics, however, came to an end in 1851 owing to the disorderly mobs which used to attend. They were however revived—including the shin beating—in 1951 for Festival of Britain year. There is satisfaction in the knowledge that the National Trust now cares for the hill which bears the name of that good old sportsman, Robert Dover. More recently the Dover Games have been revived with a torchlight procession on the Friday after Whitsun, followed the next day by the usual Scuttlebrook Wake fair.

Two miles east of Campden is a village whose name is the frequent cause of confusion among strangers and an equally frequent source of amusement to the locals; for it is as useless to inquire the way to **Ebrington** as it is to seek Yubberton on the map. The name, however, is of small importance compared with the loveliness of the village, set on the hillside so that the noon-day sun casts deep shadows from its chimneys and thatched roofs and trees, and the vale beyond seems alive with an almost luminous green. It is a village of simple thatched cottages, and on entering the church one sees with some astonishment the elab-orate tomb of Sir John Fortescue (d. 1476) wearing the robes

91

of the Lord Chief Justice, which office he filled under Henry VI, while he was lord of the manor of Ebrington.

From the top of **Ilmington Down,** there is a fresh and very lovely view of Campden nestling against the hillside. The fine tower of Campden Church looks its finest and northward the Cotswolds fall away to display the great part of wooded Warwickshire, Stratford well to the fore and the smoky haze of Birmingham beyond it. Almost below us is **Meon Hill,** like a sentry outpost guarding the hills, and lanes run down the steep hillside by Hidcote Boyce to **Mickleton,** which may be regarded as the northernmost Cotswold village. Between Hidcote Boyce and Mickleton, one mile east of the main road, is **Hidcote Bartrim.** Here is Hidcote Manor, with a beautiful garden now in the care of the National Trust. These grounds are open to the public from Easter to end-October (*daily, except Tuesdays and Fridays*); garden lovers will be attracted by the many rare plants and shrubs growing there.

# The North Cotswolds

The Oxford–Witney–Cheltenham highway is the generally accepted dividing line between the North and South Cotswolds. It is no mere arbitrary division, for the country on either side of the road is of distinctly differing type: to the north are the grand rolling hills—real Wold country—and to the south it is more abruptly carved into hill and valley, woods are more plentiful and the Cotswold influence on the architecture is less apparent the farther one travels south. Each district has its charms, but that north of the road has throughout the distinctive character and the elusive charm which provides the real Cotswold scene.

Standing near the centre of this area and commanding all its main roads, Stow-on-the-Wold claims our first attention.

### Stow-on-the-Wold

Access.—Stow is served by buses and coaches from all parts of the district.
Distances.—Banbury, 20 miles; Bourton-on-the-Water, 4; Broadway, 10; Burford, 10; Cheltenham, 18; Chipping Campden, 10; Northleach, 9; Oxford, 29; Moreton-in-Marsh, 4.
Early Closing.—Wednesday.
Hotels.—*See* p. 11.
Population.—1,737.

"Stow-on-the-Wold, where the winds blow cold"—such is the local saying; and it is noteworthy that of all the Cotswold townships the only one to disdain the shelter of valley or slope is Stow-on-the-Wold. Only the strongest reasons would lead to the use of such a site when so many more sheltered places were available, and the reasons were undoubtedly the seven important roads which meet at this point. Stow might indeed be termed the hub of the Northern Cotswolds, geographically at any rate, for roads radiate from it like the spokes of a wheel.

Yet it is by no means a characteristic example of a Cotswold town. Quite apart from the alleged bleakness of the site, it wears the remote, self-contained air that distinguishes so many

of the Northern hill-towns—less because of its architecture than from its planning, which is that of a very large open space around which buildings of all kinds are tightly packed as though to protect it, and form a great pound into which cattle could be driven for safety from raiding tribesmen. This is particularly noticeable as one comes along the Fosse Way, for the Fosse does not pass through the original Stow; most of the old buildings turn their backs on it, and so one leaves the Fosse to enter Stow. Always one has this curious feeling of *entering* Stow, as though passing through a gateway.

Whether the winds do blow colder here than elsewhere is a matter for statistics, but in summer at any rate the climatic advantages of a place some 700 feet above the sea are sufficiently obvious. It is not a large place. For years it had busy markets and two charter fairs. A deceptive appearance of importance is conveyed by the manner in which the greater number of the buildings are arranged round the large central space containing the old market-place, which is several hundred yards long. **St. Edward's Hall** (p. 95), which stands with one or two other buildings for company, replaced an older building. Across the

94

way the eye is attracted by the front of the old house known as St. Edward's.

At this end of the market-place is the Old Cross, restored in recent years, and in the shade of an old elm at the far end are the old stocks. It is when one comes to explore the size of this market-place that the reason for the site of the town becomes truly apparent. For centuries Stow was famous throughout Europe for its immense fairs, at which as many as 20,000 sheep have been sold on one occasion, and the meeting-place of roads is clearly the place for a fair. With the decline of the Cotswold wool industry, the fair changed its character, and a very considerable trade was carried on in horses, harness and farm equipment. Today however the main preoccupation of the two annual fairs, held on May 12 and October 13, is of an amusement nature.

The church is dedicated to St. Edward.

A church has existed on this site for more than a thousand years. The present church is a large and lofty building with a number of interesting points for archaeologists. The fine upstanding fourteenth-century tower, for instance, was built on the site of a Norman predecessor, yet occupies an unusual position at the east end of the south aisle. The north aisle is divided from the nave and the transept by arches of irregular span.

The chancel arch is also unusual in extending the whole width of the chancel—springing, indeed, from the north wall of the tower. The rood is, of course, modern, being a Great War Memorial. The large picture of the Crucifixion now hung in the south aisle was painted by Gaspar de Craeyer (1582–1669), contemporary and friend of Rubens and Vandyck. The roof corbels belonged to the Perpendicular roof which vanished long since, the present roof having replaced a plaster ceiling in 1859. The west window tracery is good and in recent years two of the clerestory windows have been filled with coloured glass.

After the Battle of Stow, in 1646, Sir Jacob Astley and some hundreds of his men were imprisoned in the church.

In **St. Edward's Hall** is the County Library, with a good reference section.

## EXCURSIONS FROM STOW-ON-THE-WOLD

Scenically the seven roads which radiate from Stow are among the finest in Britain. Some of the loveliest gems of the Cotswolds lie hidden in the folds of the hills westward of Stow: places which demand visit after visit, from various directions and in varying lights and seasons. Nor has one to go far afield for beauty, for hardly more than a mile or so from Stow are such villages as the Swells and the Slaughters, Icomb, and a dozen others.

### Upper and Lower Swell

The best way to come to **Upper Swell** is by the Tewkesbury road from Stow, for although it is often busy with traffic there is nothing quite like the view, as one turns over the bridge by the mill, of the great barns and trees looking down on the road as it climbs the hill. The great mill-wheel is now silent and the water diverted to flow swiftly beneath the stone bridge. Set a little back from the road near the top of the hill are the gabled manor-house, dating from 1600, and the church, the latter an unpretentious building in perfect keeping with the place.

The south porch has its ancient roof timbers and a Norman doorway and the font retains the staples with which it was fitted in the days when fonts were guarded by padlocks.

A mile south of Upper Swell and a similar distance from Stow by the Cheltenham road is **Lower Swell**, a very trim village running decorously down to the meads through which the Dikler flows to join the Windrush.

96

The little church looks down on the village from a height beside the road to Upper Swell. It is an interesting building wherein the old and the new are strangely blended, and stands on the site of a Roman crematorium. Through a Norman south door (note the carving of the Tree of Life in its tympanum) one enters the Norman nave. Note especially the small but richly detailed Norman chancel arch, opening on to a very small chancel lit by deeply splayed windows. Then one realizes that the usual arrangement of adding an aisle to an older building has here been modified so that the new work is actually the nave and instead of the little Norman chancel which has been the centre of worship here for a thousand years there is now a new chancel in the modern style. The opening through the east wall of the poor superseded nave was of course made to provide a view of the modern altar. The old Norman part of the church is now regularly used for services.

Before leaving the place, walk round the churchyard: even the newer houses up on the hill of Stow cannot rob the view of its charm: here, as in many another place, the beauty of the steep-pitched stone roofs pierced by dormers is a sheer joy.

Still travelling southward one comes in a couple of miles from Lower Swell to—

## Upper and Lower Slaughter

The name, it may be well to explain, has no sanguinary significance but is possibly derived from the Anglo-Saxon for Sloe-tree – the slaughters being "the place of the Sloes". In the days when our land was roadless, almost trackless, and had neither signposts nor milestones, travellers used natural objects to guide them on their way. The sloe trees are blackthorn bushes and a large scrub area of these bushes may have been a local landmark, as a cluster of hazel trees was at Hazleton, yews at Uley, and sapling pears at Sapperton. In Norman times, the De Sclotre family owned land here. The first of the family took his name from the place as John of Slaughter or De Sclotre.

**Upper Slaughter** is built on the hillside above the stream— a place of fine trees and grey-brown stone and quiet content. Its church is renowned for the very fine arch leading into the church from the Norman tower: the moulding is some of the best preserved to us. The chancel arch, of course, is modern work in the same style, and as with the arches, so with the fonts: one is old, the other is a modern copy. Built into the wall of the porch are fragments of ancient carving.

Upper Slaughter Manor-House is one of the most beautiful domestic buildings in the Cotswolds, with its steep-pitched roof and long line of dormers. The oldest part of the house is fifteenth-century, but the front is Elizabethan, and a very lovely picture it all makes as one follows the winding road from Upper to Lower Slaughter.

At **Lower Slaughter** the stream flows down the centre of the village, and numerous bridges, built presumably to carry the villagers from one side to the other, now seem more important as places on which to lounge gazing down into the waters at the trout lying in wait for food, or looking out beyond the end of the village to the surrounding wolds. At one point the turf bordering the stream becomes a trifle wider to form the village green, and at the Bourton end are the church and one or two larger houses, but generally speaking Lower Slaughter is a place of attractive cottages, and the ducks in the stream inevitably recall William Allingham's lines:

> " Four ducks on a pond,
> A grass bank beyond:
> A blue sky of spring,
> White clouds on the wing.
> What a little thing
> To remember for years—
> To remember with tears!"

From the Slaughters one can return along the neighbouring Fosse to Stow-on-the-Wold, though the Slaughters are nearer to Bourton-on-the-Water.

## Bourton-on-the-Water

Distances.—Stow-on-the-Wold, 4 miles; Northleach, 5; Cirencester, 15.
Early Closing.—Saturday.
Hotels.—*See* p. 10.
Population.—2,251.

It has been the fashion to allude to Bourton-on-the-Water as "the Venice of the Cotswolds", but such a comparison is misleading. Here is no network of murky waters confined between dank walls of crowded houses, but a shallow crystal stream flowing between wide verges of the greenest turf, on the edge of which are set out some of the most delightful of Cotswold houses. The stream (the Windrush) is crossed by several low bridges of graceful design, some hardly wider than a footpath and with tiny parapets. Those who have the wisdom to leave their cars and to explore the village slowly on foot will find Bourton a very admirable place, with odd and unexpected corners and many happy groupings of river, trees and the warm stone buildings.

Bourton **Church** is notable for the curious dome-like erection on its tower, and retains its original chancel of 1328. The tower dates from 1774. The nave is simple and plain. The reredos (1928) and the richly painted ceiling of the chancel repay attention, however, and in the churchyard are some curious inscriptions.

Of the **Manor-House** only a medieval dovecot remains; a more interesting feature of this kind is to be seen alongside Sherboure

99

Street, beginning at the old mill in the village. Here is a house having its face marked with holes which look as though they have been made to receive the ends of joists, but which were in fact nesting-holes for pigeons.

Of great interest in Bourton is the **Model Village** behind the *Old New Inn*, at the Rissington end of High Street. Here is a complete and remarkably accurate reproduction of Bourton itself, on the scale of one-tenth, and the builder is to be commended on the faithfulness with which he has perpetuated the characteristic details of the buildings. In the centre of the village is *Birdland*, an attractive Cotswold botanical garden, with a fine collection of birds. There is a model railway, an aquarium and a Butterfly exhibition.

Half a mile north-east of the church is **Salmonsbury Camp,** an earthwork dating from the Bronze Age.

## EXCURSIONS FROM BOURTON-ON-THE-WATER

One of the most delightful roads in the district is that running in a south-westerly direction from the centre of Bourton-on-the-Water to Farmington and Northleach. The road soon climbs, and for most of the way ascends and descends hills offering glorious views of valley and wold, with farmsteads tucked cosily in sheltered corners.

**Farmington** (p. 30) consists of a church, a comfortable-looking Georgian mansion, a few cottages and some quite imposing farm-buildings.

Farmington Church is neat and well-kept, and has not lost its charm through restoration. Electric light has been installed, but there still remain at the pew-ends the slender candlesticks which formerly illuminated the worshippers. The building dates from about 1150 and retains its chancel arch and a south doorway with a diapered tympanum. It is thought that the lintel of this doorway is Saxon. Tower and porch are fourteenth century, and several scratch-dials will be seen on the exterior.

The Georgian mansion with its stabling and dovecote is imposing. The old Rectory dates from the same period. Some cottages border on the village green which has a pumphouse originally with thatched roof. This was replaced in 1935 with a tiled roof presented by inhabitants of Farmington, Connecticut, to commemorate the founding of the American Farmington 300 years before.

Farmington is a quiet and peaceful place with wide views to the east and south. There are some new stone-built houses, but, at least for the time being, main roads have passed the village by. There is a wealth of fine trees.

From the peace of Farmington to the bustle of the main road at Northleach is little more than a mile. **Northleach** is described on pp. 31–32.

## Clapton

Below Bourton, the Dikler joins the Windrush, and together they form a considerable stream watering a very pleasant valley. On the west is **Clapton**, reached from Bourton by field-path or by a turning from the Sherborne road. Clapton is a mere handful of houses including a gabled manor and farms set, with a little church, on the hillside. The church dates from 1200 and is one of the smallest in Gloucestershire. It is fittingly simple and almost its only outstanding feature is the inscription carved on the north side of the chancel arch. It has been variously interpreted, but appears to refer to an indulgence, one version running, "Whoever shall say an Our Father and Hail Mary three times devoutly kneeling and in person, to them is a reward then and there of a thousand days."

About half a mile south of Clapton a left-hand turn from the Sherborne road is a narrow and rather rough lane, sheltered by overhanging trees for a great part of the way across the valley to the Bourton–Rissington main road.

## The Rissingtons

Three Rissingtons grace the eastern side of the valley, and of these **Great Rissington** is certainly not the least attractive. The most charming corner of Great Rissington is that in which the massive-towered church stands company with the trim manorhouse at the south-west corner of the village. The church is a well-proportioned and altogether attractive building entered by a porch into which has been built a fragment of ancient carving. Most of the structure is Early English, but there is ample evidence of a Norman predecessor—the four tower arches, for example. At the west end of the church is a series of photographs serving to remind us that tragedy penetrates even to these peaceful corners, for no fewer than five brothers from one Rissington family lost their lives in the 1914–18 War.

**Little Rissington** is built more steeply on the hillside a mile or so north from its Great neighbour. Its church stands apart from the village, on a spur from which one looks out over Bourton towards Stow-on-the-Wold. Immediately on entering, the eye is caught by the rood-loft staircase on the north side of the chancel arch and the opening to the rood (which is of course gone), and the Norman pillars and arcade between the nave and the aisle are impressive in their massive simplicity, though the westernmost one has had to be supported by an octagonal pier.

**Wyck Rissington** lies a mile or so farther northward. The most attractive approach is by the lane running almost due north; but cars have to continue up through the village to the Stow–Barrington road, where turn left for half a mile and then left again. This is a longer route than the lane mentioned above, but it has the compensation of lovely views during the steep descent to the village.

Wyck Rissington divides itself naturally into two portions: the group of houses and farms near the church and the series of cottages bordering the extensive green beside the road to the Slaughters.

The tower of the church is so massive that at first sight it seems to occupy as much ground as the nave, and its massiveness is well matched by the fine sweep of the roof, which spreads itself without a break over the nave and the north aisle. The tower is Norman work with Early English additions; possibly the base is Saxon, for there was a church here in Saxon times, and it is thought that the round-headed door

102

leading from the porch to the vestry is also Saxon. Built into the wall beside this door is an old stone inscribed:

TH
JESSER
IRLAND
MADE THIS
1618

Below it a stone with a floriated cross is believed to be part of the coffin of the man who inserted the fourteenth-century window in the choir behind the rector's stall.

The most interesting part of the church is the choir, entered by three steps. The arrangement of the windows in the east wall is very unusual, but other features are equally uncommon. In the wall at the north end of the Communion rail, for instance, is a small cistern, and over it an iron ring thought to be connected with the ancient Lenten Veil. There are several aumbries, and running round the choir wall is a stone bench which probably had some connection with the monks of Eynsham Abbey, who served the church prior to the Dissolution. The twelve lime-wood plaques hanging round the walls of the chancel are sixteenth-century Flemish work and formed part of a Rosary. The ivory picture in the nave is probably eighteenth-century German work. Note the narrow priest's door. In the south wall of the choir is a piscina with Norman moulding in Early English pattern.

The Norman font (1080) stands on a good modern base.

In the churchyard an 8-foot yew has been clipped to the shape of a cross. Adjoining the church is a maze, centred by a giant Wellingtonian Pine. Altogether it has 600 yards of path.

The Rissingtons lie along the western flank of the ridge carrying the Stow–Barrington road and to the east of this a large airfield has modernized the scene. At the north end of the ridge **Icomb Hill** above Wyck Rissington reaches almost to 800 feet above sea-level. This is a grand viewpoint, the particular feature of the foreground being the vale in which the *Evenlode* receives those tributary streams which help to transform it from a mere brook to a small river, which in turn performs almost the same service for Father Thames on a slightly larger scale.

## Icomb

Icomb was originally "Ye Combe", and as one descends to the village the appropriateness of the name is apparent. It is a sheltered, sunny little place with not too much formality in its design—good to look at and good to look from. There is a fine medieval manor-house (*private*) in the parish.

Filling the view eastward is the saddleback tower which was added to the church in the seventeenth century. There has been a church here since 1220 and possibly earlier, for it was Offa, King of Mercia, who gave Icomb to the Prior and Monks of Worcester—it has since passed to the Dean and Chapter. The chancel is good Early English work but attention is claimed by the south transept, a chantry chapel containing the tomb with effigy of Sir John Blaket (d. 1431). Notice the little "squint" over the tomb. The passage behind the south-west pier of the chapel is curious. The pulpit (modern) came from Quinton Church. Note the hour-glass by which the length of the sermon was measured.

Three miles eastward across the fields from Icomb, or easily reached from Stow by road, is—

## Bledington

The old village clusters nicely round a large green watered by one of the many local tributaries of the Evenlode, and almost opposite the *King's Head Inn* a by-road leads up to the church.

For its size this must have been—indeed it still is—an unusually handsome building, and even the good appearance of the exterior hardly prepares one for the splendid north wall of the nave, with its double tier of fifteenth-century windows adorned with canopied niches for statues and still containing ancient glass. The chancel arch is Early English; the south aisle is separated from the nave by a nicely balanced arcade partly of the Norman period, to which also the nave walls and the tub-font belong, and is connected with the chancel by a passage through what was once a chantry chapel (note the ceiling and the old glass in the window). Here, too, is a bell discarded from use, inscribed: "And Charles he is our King, 1639".

The tower fills the western end of the nave and seems to have been inserted into the original building. On the east wall are traces of mural painting and on the east of the chancel arch is some painting attributed to the thirteenth century. Other examples occur round the windows and elsewhere. Bledington Church, in short, should not be missed by those interested in old buildings. Among former incumbents of the parish was the father of Warren Hastings.

From Bledington one could make a southerly course by the site of **Bruern Abbey** to **Milton-under-Wychwood** (its name commemorates the ancient Forest of Wychwood (*see* p. 25)), or to the foot of the hills at **Idbury,** a tiny village on the hillside overlooking the Evenlode Valley. Its fine manor-house was the envy of many a Fleet Street journalist, for in these idyllic surroundings was first published *The Countryman*.

Idbury Church is to be numbered among the many in the Cotswolds which originated as simple Norman buildings, were largely reconstructed in the heyday of the wool industry and nowadays wear a somewhat forlorn air. For the Norman origin of Idbury it is necessary to look no further than the north door—it was moved to its present position in the fourteenth century. Evidence of later work (apart from the intrusive tower) is to be found in the fifteenth-century carved stone font and the screen of same date, the rood-loft entry and the large passage-squint through the pier behind the pulpit and the carved pulpit. Note also the curious brass, beside the chancel arch, to Thos. Hautin (1643).

In the churchyard, opposite the north door, is the curiously designed tomb of Sir Benjamin Baker, the celebrated engineer who is perhaps more fittingly commemorated by such of his works as the Forth Bridge.

From Idbury, lane or footpath along the hillside would bring us to pretty little **Fifield,** at the end of the lane running down from the Stow–Burford road at the curiously named *Merrymouth Inn* (6 miles from Stow). Common sense suggests leaving such an appropriate name to speak for itself, but in the interests of exactitude we have to record that in the fourteenth century the lord of the manor was John de Muremouth, a word alternatively spelt Merimuth and Mirimouth. The inn really, however, takes its name from the village, which from ancient times well into the nineteenth century was known as Fifield Merrymouth. Fifield church has an unusual octagonal tower.

# THE UPPER WINDRUSH VALLEY

## Naunton—The Guitings—Cutsdean

In its first few miles the Windrush has cut for itself a deep and narrow valley that is well wooded and in its way at least as charming as the more open stretches down by Burford. From the Fosse Bridge at Bourton-on-the-Water footpaths beside the stream can be followed to **Harford Bridge,** just below Naunton, but those forced to keep to the roads turn under the railway

105

and then bear off to the left along **Buckle Street,** which is sufficiently interesting to merit a few words to itself (*see* p. 111).

Buckle Street, however, runs along the hills sheltering the Windrush Valley on the east, and for Naunton we keep left at the fork about a mile after crossing the Stow–Andoversford road and in another mile a turn sharp left by Grange Hill Farm leads down to—

## Naunton

Coming thus to Naunton one has that familiar and most satisfying Cotswold scene—bright green of fields, against which flourishing trees impose great masses of a green that is darker and more mysterious and which heightens almost to a glow the effect of the lichened stone roofs and the sunbathed walls of the village. The ingredients of the Cotswold scene are always simple, but owing to some trick of light they produce effects here that simply cannot be matched elsewhere, and one comes down the hill to where the church stands on a little knoll beside the river. This church, like others, has been somewhat too keenly restored, but the white stone pulpit is worth seeing, and (as a reminder that Cotswold peace has been born of troublous times) one should read the monument to William Oldys, "who for his loyalty to his King and zeal for ye Established Church was barbarously murther'd by ye Rebells in ye year 1645". Another kind of association with Naunton is recalled by the brass plate recording that Clement Barksdale, author of *The Cotswold Muse*, was rector here (d. 1687).

Naunton has a fine fifteenth-century pigeon-house, with over a thousand nest-holes: not quite so handsome as that at Chastleton (p. 117), perhaps, since it is not raised on arches; but with its high gables and central lantern, very good to look upon. Unfortunately it has been allowed to lapse into disrepair.

From Naunton we follow the Andoversford road for about a mile and then turn sharply back to the right for the Windrush at one of its most delightful reaches—that beside Guiting Power. Such, at any rate, is the more usual route, but those who climb the hill on the north side at Naunton and come down to the

Windrush through the woods of Guiting Grange will not regret the greater labour of this route. In any case, only about 3 miles separate the two villages.

## Guiting Power,

or **Lower Guiting**, is built irregularly around a green on the westward slopes of the valley: a mere handful of cottages, but such cottages as delight the heart of artists: roofs, chimneys, dormers and gables stand out at all angles, each delightful in itself and each contributing to form a memorable picture of a typical Cotswold village; even though the area round the upper green, with its beautiful chestnut tree, bears the name "Piccadilly". In Well Lane stands the Old Bake House, built in 1603 but now converted as modern residences.

The church lies at the south end of the village, withdrawn from the road among barns and trees; apart from its splendid Norman work it bears testimony to one of those increasingly rare events—a loving restoration. Originally the church consisted merely of a Norman nave, to which a chancel was added in the twelfth to thirteenth century, and during the fifteenth century the excellent roof was put on. During last century the transepts were added, and more recently the church has been restored—with what care is indicated by the notice beside the Norman priest's door and the adjoining small window in the chancel, "At the restoration of 1903 these were not disturbed." But the best

features of the church are the fine Norman doorways, particularly that on the south side with a sacred chalice incised on its tympanum. The "inverted chalice" was the emblem of the Knights Templar. In the churchyard, one stone dated 1602 bears at its foot a small carved skull and crossbones.

The village can be recommended to those in search of a headquarters for good walks and excursions off the high roads. There is, for example, a grand lane climbing up among the hills to **Roel Gate**—which in the beauty and extent of its views is a gateway indeed. A turning from this lane climbs up past Guiting Wood and so down past Sudeley to Winchcombe; others go to **Hawling** and, on the other side of the valley, to that most excellent artery Buckle Street.

The Stanway road continues up the valley to **Barton**—a farming hamlet built on hillsides of such steepness as to have the quality of cliffs—and **Kineton**, a roadside village with unexpected charms for those who turn down to the right to where the river is crossed by fords as it flows among the trees. Beside the lower ford is an ancient stone bridge formed of two immense slabs of stone—very much on the lines of the Dartmoor clapper bridges. Lanes lead out of either side of the valley, which attains its greatest richness at—

## Temple Guiting

Set among trees down beside the river, the village is so secluded that a stranger may never be quite sure if he has seen every part of it: certain it is that a great proportion of those who ride along the adjacent main road have no idea of the beauty that lies at their elbow, notwithstanding the charm of the views through the trees and across the park. This valley of the infant Windrush has endless joys and endless beauties. It is all on a diminutive scale but its call is insistent; and time and again one climbs the hills on either side to make a long excursion over the wolds, only to find oneself turning back, foregoing the sweeping views of the uplands for the delight of making a quiet and leisurely way through the woods of this valley, so crowded is it with intimate beauty.

The name of Temple Guiting commemorates the fact that it

formed part of the properties given by Gilbert de Lacy in the twelfth century to the Order of Templars. Nothing is left of the preceptory from which they managed their estates, though there are slight remains of the numerous mills which were once a feature of the valley and which probably had their origin under this management.

The chancel of the church is twelfth-century Norman, with a priest's door on the north side and a low side window in the south-west corner; there is Flemish glass in one of the nave windows. The majority of the Perpendicular windows were given a classical shape by the Rev. George Talbot, a wealthy 18th-century vicar, who built Temple Guiting House. Much of his work was destroyed in 1885 but his beautiful pulpit, and the splendid royal arms of George II on the West wall remain.

At the adjacent manor farmstead is another of these charming pigeon-houses of which those at Naunton and Lower Slaughter have already been noted. This at Temple Guiting is remarkable for the way in which it is built into the house itself: only the cupola-doorway above the roof indicates its real purpose.

Following the ever-narrowing valley northward from Temple Guiting we come to **Ford**, a hamlet where the road from Stow and Upper Swell comes down to cross the infant Windrush.

**Cotswold Farm Park** (*mid-May–Sept., daily fee*). Reached from Ford, on the road to Stow-on-the-Wold, and turning right towards Bourton-on-the-Water at the first crossroads, we come after a mile to Bemborough Farm on the right where is the Cotswold Farm Park. This is not a wild life reserve, but a research centre for the preservation of rare breeds of farm animals. Here are one of the few surviving flocks of Cotswold sheep, some of the Old Gloucester cattle, and many almost extinct breeds from other parts of the British Isles. Here too, in 1973, was born the first native reindeer on the Cotswolds for over 1000 years.

At Ford our Windrush pilgrimage is nearly at an end, for although the stream can be traced a little further, it is generally accounted to have its source at **Cutsdean.** This little village is well-seen from the south for it is perched high on an escarpment above the river. The village appears a curious blend of neglect and new building, and has an air that possibly arises from its site but which definitely differentiates it from other Cotswold villages. It lies high, for the summit of Cutsdean Hill, a mile eastward, is over 1,000 feet above the sea.

Continuing by the road running due north from Ford, and leaving Cutsdean on the right, one comes after a few miles to **Snowshill**, an attractive and secluded hill-village. Just beyond the church, and on the left of the road is **Snowshill Manor**, a Tudor house now in the charge of the National Trust (*see* p. 82). Two miles further on one passes the church of St. Eadburgha (p. 84), and soon reaches **Broadway** (p. 83).

An alternative route from Ford is to take the road running eastward to **Stow-on-the-Wold**, crossing Buckle Street (*see* p. 111) near the woods of Trafalgar, a mile or so east of which is—

### Condicote

Condicote, for those who come to it from the main road, and seen across the fields, looks just another large farm with attendant cottages. The community is mainly occupied with farming and there are stables for racehorses and hunters. Well-cultivated fields are to be seen on either hand, and the village green is also walled around like a great pound. At the western end of the green is an ancient cross—which has stood here since the fourteenth century.

Condicote Church is a simple village church, which although restored in 1889, is surprisingly rich in Norman work. One enters by a fine south door to be faced with a chancel arch scarcely less interesting. The walls and the piers of the arch have borne their load for so many centuries, however, that they lean appreciably from the perpendicular. The walls, nevertheless, are of considerable thickness and appear to be in no danger of collapse.

Another surprise awaits those who leave the main road a mile nearer Swell, for **Donnington Brewery**, down in the valley, is about as peaceful a scene of industry as one could imagine. Originally it was a mill, and it is the fine old mill-wheel which supplies power to the brewery, the water being gathered into a huge pool set between green banks so that the whole makes a very memorable picture.

The village of **Donnington**, some 2 miles east, has a place in history, for here Lord Astley, on his way to join the King at Oxford with 3,000 men, laid down his arms. "Being taken captive and wearyed in this fight, and being ancient (for old ages silver haires had quite covered over his head and beard), the Souldiers brought him a Drum to sit and rest himselfe upon; who, being sate, he said (as was most credibly enformed) unto our soldiers: Gentlemen, yee may now sit downe and play, for you have done all your worke, if you fall not out among yourselves."

A little northwest is **Longborough** a picturesque village about a mile from the Fosse Way. Like that at Condicote, its church has a fine Norman south doorway. Much of the building is fourteenth century, including a fine window in the south transept.

## BY BUCKLE STREET TO BROADWAY

**Buckle Street** is one of those long, straight and ancient ways which march so purposefully from point to point, regardless of what lies on either hand, that they present a unique cross-section of the district traversed. Buckle Street begins at Bourton-on-the-Water, and for much of its length is suitable for cars; other parts are rougher and on certain short stretches you are unlikely to meet any wheeled vehicle other than a farm cart. It leaves the Fosse Way just north of the bridge over the Windrush at Bourton, throws a glance at Upper Slaughter, crosses the Stow–Andoversford road, takes the right fork where the left is signposted to Naunton, and passes high above the Guitings. Thence it continues along the high ground, reaching its highest point at **Cutsdean Hill**, 1,000 feet above sea-level. East of Snowshill it deteriorates to a track for a few hundred yards, but once fairly launched on its way up the hill it is again the pleasant road which is its main characteristic all the way to **Broadway Tower** (p. 85). After rather tortuously by-passing **Saintbury,** the ancient Buckle Street continues its straight, northerly course to the Honeybournes and Bidford-on-Avon.

111

# The North-east Cotswolds

## Oxford to Moreton-in-Marsh and Broadway

For the first few miles from Oxford the scenery is rather suburban, but as we approach Woodstock long stretches of dry-walling remind us that here too we are on the threshold of the real Cotswold country.

### Woodstock and Blenheim

**Access.**—By bus and coach from Oxford, Chipping Norton, Stratford-upon-Avon, etc.
**Distances.**—Oxford, 8; Chipping Norton, 12; Witney, 8; Stratford-upon-Avon, 32; Bicester, 12; London, 61.
**Early Closing.**—Wednesday.
**Hotels.**—*Bear, Marlborough Arms, Pied Bull, Dorchester.*
**Population.**—2,070.

**Woodstock** (*Wudestoc*, the "woody place") was of old a royal hunting-lodge on the east border of a forest some 12 miles in diameter. It is rich in associations. Here Alfred is stated to have completed his translation of Boëthius. Here Ethelred issued an ordinance forbidding the sale of Christian men. Here Henry I collected a menagerie. Here, too, Henry II used to come and visit Fair Rosamund, daughter of Walter, Lord Clifford. Her well is still to be seen, but the tower and maze have vanished. The story throws a curious light on the morality of those times. The King used to come with his whole suite, and waste lands were granted that accommodation might be found for them. For their convenience he provided a market every Tuesday, and thereto he added a Fair of three days on the Feast of St. Matthew. It was at Woodstock, too, that Becket first broke with the King.

Richard I repaired to Woodstock to recoup after his experience of an Austrian prison, and John to recover from the effects of signing Magna Charta. Henry III signed the treaty with the Welsh princes at Woodstock, and Edward the Black Prince was born at Praunce's Place in the borough. The Queen's Pool, named after his royal mother, is still to be seen. Later, Woodstock was the scene of the temporary imprisonment of Elizabeth by Mary,

**Lower Slaughter** (*R. Westlake*)

**Chipping Campden** (*Eagle*)

**Slad Valley** (*Eagle*)

**Moreton-in-Marsh** (*Eagle*)

and in the next century the manor-house was much affected by the Stuarts. After Blenheim, its connection with royalty ceased. The names of great commoners connected with Woodstock are, probably, Chaucer, who should have frequented the place, and, certainly, Speaker Lenthall. In 1302 and 1305 the town returned a Member to Parliament, but after that date came a long hiatus, even up to the reign of Mary. Nevertheless, in the time of Henry VI, Woodstock had risen to be a borough of importance, with a Mayor, Sergeant-at-Mace and Corporation. During the Parliamentary War Woodstock was taken and retaken. Many of the archives survive, and very quaint some are. One records that for every sermon preached a bottle of wine was presented to the preacher.

The Church (St. Mary Magdalene) is too often overlooked. It is, however, well worth visiting, and is quite an interesting study of the development from Norman architecture by Early English and Decorated to Perpendicular. Its rich Norman doorway in the south wall should be noticed. The church suffered somewhat from a restoration in 1878.

## Blenheim Palace

**Admission.**—The Palace and Gardens are open to the public from April to October, daily from 11.30 a.m. to 5 p.m. Charge. Car park, fee. Teas served on the Terrace. Friday is connoisseurs day when charge differs.

Magnificent were the services rendered to the nation and Europe by John Churchill, Duke of Marlborough, and magnificent is the Palace of Blenheim which commemorates them. Parliament granted an enormous sum, close on a quarter of a million, for the work, and it cannot be said that the architect, Sir John Vanbrugh, wasted a shilling of it. Blenheim is a splendid example of Italian Renaissance work. Brown, the landscape gardener, sometimes called "Capability", sometimes other names, caught the inspiration, and the grounds are worthy of the building. Specially notable is the lake formed by damming the little River Glyme.

The old Royal Manor-House was swept away on the building of Blenheim, and the only survival of the old Forest ways is the glove trade. Woodstock gloves are famous and of characteristic design, and there is no reasonable doubt that the industry has come down in direct descent from the times when the villagers used to fashion gloves from the pelts of deer hunted in the royal forest.

Beyond Woodstock the road proceeds by long sweeping hills through **Enstone** and near **Heythorp** to—

## Chipping Norton

Distances.—Banbury, 13 miles; Burford, 11; Cheltenham, 28; Oxford, 19; London, 75; Moreton-in-Marsh, 8; Stow-on-the-Wold, 10.
Early Closing.—Thursday.
Golf.—9-hole course beside Oxford Road.
Hotels.—*See* p. 10.
Market Day.—Wednesday.
Population.—5,020.

The town stands on the southern slopes of a valley carved by one of the numerous tributaries of the Evenlode; it is the highest town in Oxfordshire and one of the most picturesque. The first part of the name refers to the market which was held here from very early times, and which doubtless influenced the width of the main streets. At either end of the market-place are

the **Town Hall**, in the Classical style, and the **Old Guildhall**, a building of much greater appeal which is now used for local government offices. At the back of the Town Hall, a pillar of the old Market Hall was re-erected in 1955; the stone at the base is part

114

of the old wayside cross. In Church Street a picturesque group of almshouses (A.D. 1640) stands just above the **Parish Church.**

This is a Perpendicular building, entered by an unusual hexagonal porch, vaulted and with a sundial high on its southern face. The fine clerestory windows and nave pillars were installed about 1500. The lovely tracery of the East window of the south aisle is of fourteenth-century date. There is a hagioscope on the south wall of the north chancel aisle, and the church is interesting for the possession of two north aisles. In the outer one are preserved a number of brasses chiefly of the fifteenth and sixteenth centuries.

Lining its wide streets are several attractive eighteenth-century buildings. Chipping Norton has always been connected with the woollen industry, and the weaving of tweed material is still carried on.

**Castle Banks** beyond the church are grassy mounds marking the site of a former castle.

**Churchill**, 2½ miles south-west of Chipping Norton, was the birthplace of Warren Hastings (*see* p. 116) and also of William Smith "the father of British Geology".

Descending the hill below Chipping Norton Church and climbing again with good views (including the local tweed mill) to the left, we come by way of **Salford** to the *Cross Hands Inn*, where we turn to the right for—

### The Rollright Stones

Enclosed by railings are two groups of stones, known as the **Circle,** the **Whispering Knights** and, on the other side of the road, the solitary **King Stone**. The soft nature of the stone suggests that formerly the monoliths were considerably more imposing. As to their origin and purpose there are a number of theories, but their position on the brow of a hill, which is also a wonderful viewpoint, suggests at least an affinity of idea with such barrows as Belas Knap and Hetty Pegler's Tump.

Popular superstition, unhampered by the need for accuracy, is at no loss to account for the stones. Tradition tells how a king set out to conquer England and as he came up the hill from the village of Great Rollright and behind the grand view over Little Compton, he was halted by a witch who instructed him to take "Seven long strides" and then—

> "If Long Compton thou canst see,
> King of England thou shalt be."

Such an easy victory had not probably occurred to the King, who cried:

"Stick, stock, stone
As King of England I shall be known."

Eagerly he turned off the road towards the crest of the hill—but as he took the seventh stride he found himself faced not by Long Compton but by the long mound of earth which still remains. Then spake the witch:

"As Long Compton thou canst not see
King of England thou shalt not be.
Rise up stick, and stand still, stone,
For King of England thou shalt be none.
Thou and thy men hoar stones shalt be,
And I shall be an eldern-tree."

And even as the witch pronounced these words the King turned into a stone and his army across the road likewise became monoliths, while the witch became an elder tree, though it would seem that the old lady delayed her transformation until she had also made stones of the Whispering Knights, who had lagged behind the rest of the army and were plotting treason.

As for the name, A. J. Evans pointed out long ago that "Rollright, which appears in Domesday as Rollandri, is just a corruption of Rollanriht—the jurisdiction of Roland the Brave, the legendary champion of Christianity. . . "

From the high ground occupied by the Rollright Stones, we can not only survey Long Compton but, not having encountered a witch, can make a way down to that village with old houses along the main road and with a pleasant surprise in the shape of a lych-gate having above it a little room roofed with thatch. Hence one could come to Moreton-in-Marsh by way of Little Wolford, notable for a charming sixteenth-century manor-house. Originally there were two projecting wings, one at either end of the hall, but only one remains, and with its half-timbered upper storey a very delightful picture it makes.

Alternatively, from the Rollright Stones one could retrace the way along the ridge to the *Cross Hands* and thence keep straight ahead along the Stow road, descending to the Evenlode at Adlestrop, with its fine mansion in a wooded park, opposite which is Daylesford, memorable for its association with Warren Hastings.

Let Macaulay tell how when only seven years old young Hastings "lay on the bank of the rivulet which flows through the old domain of his house to join the Isis. There, as threescore and ten years later he told the tale, rose in his mind a scheme which, through all the turns of

116

his eventful career, was never abandoned. He would recover the estate which had belonged to his fathers. He would be Hastings of Daylesford." Macaulay's pages, too, will tell how in 1788 he achieved his desire, buying the estate, rebuilding the house and settling down to the life of a country gentleman. When he died in 1818 he was buried in the neighbouring churchyard, but his grave now lies below the altar of the church, which was built in 1860 and specially extended to cover the spot.

Two miles north-east of Daylesford, and in the angle formed by the road we have followed and that from the *Cross Hands* to Moreton, stands—

## Chastleton House

Open daily except Wednesdays. 10.30–1 and 2–5.30 or dusk; Sundays, 2–5. Fee. Refreshments by arrangement.

Chastleton House is in the very best sense of the word a "show-place". Built in 1603 by Walter Jones, a Witney wool-merchant, who bought the estate from Robert Catesby, the Gunpowder Plotter, it is imposing without and—to most people—a surprise within, for it is lavishly furnished and adorned in the best seventeenth-century style: china, tapestries, furniture and, of course, panelling which includes a secret chamber. But perhaps the most poignant relic is the Bible owned by Charles I and used by him on the scaffold. That the secret chamber is no modern invention is proved by the adventure which befell a member of the family who fled here from Worcester's fatal field in 1651.

Hardly had he reached the house when the sound of his pursuers' horses was heard, and in due course their knock thundered upon the door and they demanded entrance in the name of the Parliament, adding that they were searching for a fugitive whom it appeared they identified with the King himself. The fugitive meanwhile had hidden himself in the hiding-place in the bedroom; but can hardly have felt comforted when his pursuers announced their intention of spending the night at Chastleton and of sleeping in that same room! However, Mrs. Jones took matters in hand, and in preparing supper for her unwelcome guests managed to mix enough laudanum with the wine to ensure that they would sleep well, and while they slept her husband slipped from his hiding-place and escaped from the house.

The great house is so overpowering that one can easily forget that Chastleton has other beauties to show. The delightful box garden dates from 1700 and there is a charming little dovecot in the fields across the road; raised on four arches and with high gables and a central cupola or lantern, it is a memorial of the days when a well-populated pigeon-house was an important factor in catering.

Chastleton, in addition, has a very fine barn—one of those typical Cotswold barns which are far more impressive in their simple mass than the most ornate of churches.

Regaining the main road opposite the turning to **Little Compton,** we resume the journey to Moreton-in-Marsh, passing in a mile or so under trees at the corner of the Wolford road, the pillar known as the **Four Shire Stone** marking the meeting-place of Gloucestershire, Warwickshire, and Oxfordshire. Formerly the stone marked the conjunction of the Worcestershire boundary also, but this line was altered around 1928.

## Moreton-in-Marsh

Access.—Coaches from most parts of the district during the season. *Station* on Oxford–
    Evesham line (Western Region).
Early Closing.—Wednesday.
Hotels.—*See* p. 10.
Population.—2,477.

Whether Moreton-in-Marsh derived its name from its situation among low-lying ground, or from its position close to the march or boundary between Gloucestershire and Oxfordshire, is a matter which may well be left to the experts, most visitors being content to regard it as a pleasant little town built almost entirely along either side of an exceptionally wide main street—part of the Fosse Way—in which its handsome Hall stands in dignified isolation. This is known as the **Redesdale Hall** and was donated by Lord Dulverton to the Rural Council in 1951.

Moreton is old, as its situation on the Fosse would imply, but except for the little **Curfew Tower** opposite the Market Hall it has little of antiquity to show, though parts of its thirteenth-century **Church** of St. David have been incorporated in the new church built during last century. This church is worth visiting.

In the Curfew Tower is the original curfew bell which was tolled up to 1860. The tree-lined streets have pleasant old Cotswold houses and inns. At the *White Hart* in the High Street, Charles I lodged for a night in July 1644. The manor-house at the Stow end of the main street is now an hotel. The old stone building dates from the sixteenth century. Remains of a secret passage leading to the church three hundred yards away may still be seen. There is a beautiful garden and orchard.

Included in the parish is **Batsford**, reached from Moreton by a tree-lined road to the north-west. The charming church is beautifully situated near the entrance to Batsford Park wherein are many rare trees and shrubs. Moreton is within reach of some very good scenery indeed, as those know who have followed the westward road to—

## Bourton-on-the-Hill

Bourton-on-the-Hill, formerly Burton Henmershe, is a village of some 250 people. It was earlier split between two manors and still has two manor houses, that at the upper end having belonged until the nineteenth century to Westminster Abbey. Its cottages and the church sit happily on the steep hillside, the gardens, a feature of the place, hang before them like a series of huge window-boxes. The quarries above the village are known to have been worked since the fifteenth century. The second manor-house, at the foot of the village, has a large stone tithe-barn dated 1570.

The **Church,** in its trim rose-adorned churchyard, is clean and cool, but has few objects of archaeological interest apart from the Norman

119

pillars of the nave arcade and the font, which was buried in the church-yard at the Reformation and on being dug up was cut to fit against one of the pillars. This continued until 1894 when it was restored and placed in its present position. The interior furnishings of the church also date from this period.

Another item of interest is the Winchester Bushel and Peck which is kept in the church. In 1587 Queen Elizabeth granted a Charter to the City of Winchester with a new set of weights and measures. These measures were fixed upon for the invariable rule and standard of the whole Kingdom, and being made by the Queen's special direction on purpose for this city they thereby acquired the denomination of the Standard or Winchester Measure, which was enforced by Act of Parliament down to their abolition in the reign of William IV. Stewards of Manors and Clerks to Magistrates were directed by statute to provide themselves with these standard measures for use in disputes relating to corn rents and collection of tithes.

These measures are dated 1816 and are made of bell metal; after various vicissitudes they were recovered for the Church in 1931.

The road between Bourton-on-the-Hill and Stow-on-the-Wold passes **Sezincote,** notable for a house built in the Hindu style by Sir Charles Cockerell, of the East India Company, which house so moved the Prince Regent to envy that he determined to go one better. The result was the Brighton Pavilion. In this connection it is worth noting that although the first plans for the Indian-ization of the Pavilion were the work of Repton, who was landscape gardener at Sezincote, the final plans were drawn up by his partner, the famous Nash. Sezincote also has links with that Sir Thomas Overbury whose death (1613) by slow poisoning in the Tower of London is still remembered.

On reaching the top of Bourton-on-the-Hill, a turning to the right leads to Blockley, passing **Bourton Wood** on the left. Although many of the old forest trees have been felled and re-placed by new plantations, largely of conifer, some ancient oaks and fine beeches still remain. The road drops steeply into **Blockley** village, clustered round the ancient Church with its handsome tower rebuilt after damage in the Great Storm of 1703, and its south porch with sundial, sheltering a Norman door. The interior contains a good Jacobean pulpit, brasses, some fine monumental busts to the Rushouts by Rysbrack and others, and

120

a quaint wall-monument to a lady of the Childe family. The Bishops of Worcester were formerly Lords of the Manor and had a palace here in early times.

Stone cottages poised here and there on the steep sides of the valley, in picturesque informality, look down on streams which once turned many mill-wheels when women and children throwsted silk for Coventry ribbon-weavers. The mills have been converted into delightful houses.

The village claims to be one of the first to be lit by electricity, which was installed in 1887.

At the Dovedale end of High Street, there stands in the garden of Fish Cottage (*private*), a stone inscribed:

IN MEMORY

OF THE

OLD FISH.

UNDER THE SOIL

THE OLD FISH DO LIE

20 YEARS HE LIVED

AND THEN DID DIE

HE WAS SO TAME

YOU UNDERSTAND

HE WOULD COME AND

EAT OUT OF OUR HAND

DIED APRIL THE 20TH 1855

AGED 20 YEARS.

From Blockley we can regain the Moreton – Bourton – Broadway road *via* Greenway (signposted for Broadway) at one of the most charming parts of the avenue-like **Five Mile Drive**, with glimpses on the right of Campden (*see* p. 87) and then, on the left, through the trees, to Broadway Tower. One can never tire of this road, busy as it is, for although the views from it are negligible in extent they have everywhere a suggestion of untold beauties and riches just over the brow of the hill. An enticing highway, the Five Mile Drive, and fittingly it brings us to the *Fish Inn* and the magnificent panorama from the top of **Broadway Hill** (*see* p. 84).

# Cirencester

The excellent touring centre of Cirencester, the "capital of the Cotswolds", has developed from the *Corinium Dobunnorum* of Roman times. With the advent of the Saxons, the name became Cirenceaster and finally Cirencester. In Elizabethan days it was referred to as Ciceter. Today the pronunciation of the name is Cirencester.

The earliest reference to the district is that it was occupied by the British tribes known as the *Dobunni*. Jewellery and other relics of this age have been found in a burial mound on Birdlip Hill. With the Roman invasion of A.D. 43, this British settlement was made a military post on the Ermin Street and soon became a focal point linking the great Roman roads (Fosse Way and Akeman Street) of the countryside. Here the new town of Corinium grew up and rapidly expanded, until, with the exception of London, it was the largest city in Britain. Defences were erected with gates and stone ramparts. Considerable remains of these have been excavated. The walls remained almost intact until the fourteenth century after which they were gradually demolished.

Within the city, the Romans built fine temples, houses with exquisite sculpture and mosaic floors, a colonnaded Forum and a Basilica.

There is little to be seen of Corinium above ground today, but remains of Roman buildings are still being uncovered. The Museum contains the outstanding floor mosaics from Dyer Street (1849) and the recent discoveries from Beeches Road (1971). A short length of Roman town wall has been excavated and restored in the Abbey Grounds; outside the line of the defences is the large amphitheatre, used for public entertainments and spectacles. It is locally called the Bull Ring and is accessible to visitors.

After the departure of the Romans, Corinium was plundered and burnt by the Saxons in 577, but owing to its valuable position on important road junctions, it was never entirely deserted. A new Saxon town gradually took shape on the ruins of the Roman city, and is mentioned in Anglo-Saxon chronicles of the tenth century as a "Royal City" and King Canute presided over a great council here in 1020. Under Norman rule, Cirencester became increasingly important. A castle was built—probably near the Park—and a great Abbey founded by Henry I in 1117 immediately to the north of the present Parish Church. The castle was so utterly destroyed by King Stephen *circa* 1138 during the civil war with Matilda that no trace of it remains.

So, too, with the great **Abbey** which dominated the life of the town from the twelfth century down to the Dissolution in 1534, after which the buildings were sold to Roger Bassinge on condition that "all edifices within the site and precincts shall be pulled down and carried away". Bassinge did his work so well that today only what is known as the Hospital Gate remains of the Abbey which at its fall had an annual income amounting to the very considerable sum (in those days) of £1,051 7s. 1½d. and which in its heyday was "absolute master of the town and its trade, and was entitled to nip in the bud every attempt to cultivate independence or develop autonomy. . . . The Abbot blessed you as rector of the parish church. Your grain had to be ground at his mills on the Churn, and if you were hanged it was upon his gallows and at his orders." (*Baddeley.*)

Of the **Parish Church** the Abbot was merely rector, so that when disaster fell upon the Abbey it passed by the great building which, like so many others described in this Guide, forms the principal monument to the local magnitude of the Cotswold wool trade and the munificence of the wool-staplers. Yet even the church was not allowed to dream in peace of the great days, and those less great, which it had seen pass over the town: the nave was rebuilt and the porch was rebuilt, so that although so many centuries have passed since Corinium was founded, and though so much that might be found is buried under more modern buildings, it is still the Roman civilization which has left the principal mementoes in Cirencester. That so many of these have been gathered into the local museum, and are protected by glass cases, in no way lessens their significance as evidence of the importance of Corinium; rather does their grouping and labelling enable us to understand what manner of men and women it was who knew the place more than fifteen hundred years ago.

If only for this reason, most visitors make their way first to—

## The Corinium Museum

The museum is in Park Street, and is open weekdays, and Sundays, June–August. In 1938 the purpose-built museum building was erected in the garden of Abberley House, to contain the amalgamated collections of Roman antiquities found in and around Cirencester, formed respectively by the 4th Earl Bathurst and Major and Mrs. Wilfrid Cripps. Through the generosity of both families the Bathurst and Cripps collections (previously housed in separate private museums) were presented to the town, together with Abberley House, the fine 18th-century building in Park Street.

This is no ordinary local museum, but one of the highest interest and importance to those interested in the Roman occupation of Britain. In addition to tessellated pavements, here are sculptures, pottery and bronzes; an altar to the Suleae or Suleviae: a medicine stamp, which bears the name of an eye specialist and his prescriptions for ocular disorders. There are also a large number of personal ornaments, articles of toilet and other similar witnesses to the kind of life led by the inhabitants of Corinium. Visitors interested in word puzzles will be attracted by a five-line word square incised on a fragment of wall-plaster from a Roman house concealing the Christian invocation, *Pater Noster*.

```
R O T A S
O P E R A
T E N E T
A R E P O
S A T O R
```

## The Parish Church

This was built in Norman times to replace a Saxon church demolished to make room for the abbey—and Norman work is still to be seen. The nave was twice rebuilt—in the twelfth

124

century and again in the sixteenth—and the fifteenth and sixteenth centuries (the heyday of the Cotswold wool industry) saw also the rebuilding of the east end and the erection of the tower (1400) which is so fine a feature not only of the building itself but in many a distant view of the town.

The church is a magnificent structure of graceful proportions and a wealth of carving. The elaborate South Porch—a rebuilding of that erected in 1500—has beautiful fan-vaulting. Entering the nave from this doorway, we note a figure of a Blue Coat Boy on the wall to the right. This was formerly used as an alms box for the schools. To the left is some fifteenth-century ecclesiastical embroidery.

Like those at Northleach and Chipping Campden, Cirencester Church is notable for the window in the east end of the nave, above the chancel arch, but of the three, Cirencester's window is easily the most graceful and has less suggestion of having been in the nature of an afterthought. By contrast the tall narrow chancel arch is very effective. This window, too, sets off very well the nave roof, from which the eye drops to the clerestory and the splendid series of arches springing so easily from the pillars which support them.

The great cross above the rood-screen is modern, but the screen mostly dates from the fifteenth century, as do the sidescreens. The pulpit dates from the early sixteenth century, though the colour has been renewed. It is of the "wine-glass" shape familiar in many Gloucestershire churches: its open tracery is probably unique.

In the chancel, the east window is filled with fifteenth-century glass—the seraphim-bearing shields were formerly in the Chapel of St. Edmund (or Garstang chapel).

Separated from the nave by a stone screen is **Trinity Chapel**, with a magnificent fifteenth-century roof. The cost of the chapel was mainly defrayed by William Prelatte and Richard Dixton, whose brasses are among those still to be seen here. The Yorkist badge, so prominent over every arch in the chapel, was added in compliment to Richard, Duke of York, of whom Prelatte and Dixton were followers.

125

The adjacent Lady Chapel contains interesting brasses and a monument to Samuel Rudder—the Gloucestershire historian. The round-headed doorway is the original outer door of the Norman church.

A squint or hagioscope looks towards the High Altar both from the Lady Chapel and from the adjoining **St. Katherine's Chapel,** with a very fine stone-groined roof and a series of wall paintings: that on the north wall showing St. Christopher, while St. Katherine appears on the south wall, and at the west end of the north wall are shown incidents in the life of St. Nicholas, to whom with St. Katherine the chapel was dedicated.

South of the chancel is the **Chapel of St. John the Baptist,** now used to house the organ and as a choir vestry, but with features of interest in the fresco displaying the Plantagenet badge—stars and crescents, and a monument to George Monox, in office as Sheriff of London in Charles I's time. Note the Norman window built up on the nave side of the west wall.

Enclosed by a beautiful screen in the adjacent corner of the south aisle is the **Chapel of St. Edmund of Canterbury,** established by the Garstang family. The church possesses a beautiful collection of Elizabethan plate which can be seen on application to the vicar.

In an angle, near the north-west corner of the church, is the **Old High Cross,** the old town market-cross. For many years it stood in Earl Bathurst's Park; in its present position it has the advantage of the background provided by the grey old walls of the church.

From time to time the church is referred to as "the Abbey Church"; but this is incorrect, for although the abbot was also rector of the Parish Church, the two establishments were quite distinct, which is as well, for though we can still rejoice in the Parish Church, the **Abbey** is represented by a solitary gateway which may be seen by taking the first right-hand turning out of Gloucester Street (Spitalgate Lane) and turning right again into Grove Lane.

Spitalgate Lane takes its name from the **Hospital of St. John the Evangelist,** founded by Henry I but now represented only by what appears to be part of the chapel. On the other (the west) side of Gloucester Street, in Thomas Street, is the **Hospital of St. Thomas** or **The Weavers' Hall,** founded in the fifteenth century by Sir William Nottingham for the shelter of four poor weavers and in continuous occupation since.

A walk through the town is full of interest and surprises.

There are the old inns—the *Fleece, Crown, Bear, King's Head* and the *Black Horse*, all containing much old work.

There are delightful old houses, such as that now occupied by Lloyd's Bank in Castle Street, and others can be seen in Coxwell Street and Gloucester Street. In the latter is the old School House and the site of the old theatre where Kemble, Macready and Mrs. Siddons have acted. Dollar Street is a corruption of Dole Hall Street, for here stood the Almoner's gate to the Abbey. Cecily Hill has a charming collection of houses, except for the mock castle at the end—now the Barracks.

## Public Buildings

The Offices of Cotswold District Council are in Dyer Street, next to the **Bingham Library,** a branch of the Gloucestershire County Library. The original foundation of the library was made by Daniel George Bingham, a native of Cirencester who lived and worked much of his life in Utrecht. In its Lait Gallery exhibitions are displayed from time to time.

Also of interest to visitors are two recent additions to the town, the **Barn Theatre,** used for theatrical performances, dances and

receptions, and the social and cultural centre known as **The Beeches**.

A little outside the town, between the Fosse Way and the road to Stroud stands the **Royal Agricultural College** which was founded in 1846 and for many years has taken a leading part in the advancement of scientific agriculture.

South of the town flooded gravel pits have been converted into a centre for water sports, yachting, water-skiing and winter sports.

### The Park

Open daily. No cars, cycles or dogs.

The magnificent park of 3,000 acres belongs to the Earl Bathurst. The estate originally belonged to the Abbey, but came into the possession of the Bathurst family in 1690. The present mansion in the grounds was built in the early eighteenth century and probably incorporates part of an earlier Elizabethan house. The house with its gardens and lake are strictly private and the public are not allowed access. Protecting the house on the eastern side and visible from Park Street is a wonderful yew hedge, over 30 feet in height.

The public entrance is by the park gates at Cecily Hill—five minutes' walk from the market-place *via* Blackjack Street and Park Street. Immediately facing the entrance is the Broad Ride, a fine avenue 150 feet wide and stretching, with one diversion, over 5 miles to Sapperton. In the Park are several ornamental buildings, including **Pope's Seat**. Pope was a regular visitor.

There is considerable farmland in the Park, as well as acres of forestry which maintains the original landscape layout of 1715. On Boxing Day and other hunting days there is a splendidly colourful meet attended by many riders and foot followers. During the summer, Polo is played every Sunday afternoon by Cirencester Park Polo Club. Immediately beside the Ivy Lodge Polo Ground a Leisure Area has been opened. The entrance to this Leisure area and Polo ground is off the A419 Cirencester–Stroud road, 2 miles from Cirencester.

**Cirencester** (*Vyner*)

**Painswick** (*Eagle*)

Stroud (*Eagle*)

Chipping Sodbury (*Eagle*)

# EXCURSIONS FROM CIRENCESTER

Sapperton lies 5 miles from Cirencester and the pedestrian route is through glades, fields and by woodland paths to the junction of many avenues known as "Ten Rides" from where the walk leads in another mile or so to Sapperton Park. Beyond the lodge, at the point where a road crosses the avenue, turn right and then take the first turn on the left to—

## Sapperton

Sapperton is gloriously placed at the head of the **Golden Valley** on a hillside so steep that the church spire shows over the tree-tops below one.

This church is something of a surprise to those accustomed to the familiar Cotswold type, for it is a building largely remodelled in the reign of Queen Anne, and instead of stone the carving is in wood. It is, in fact, unusually rich in woodwork, old and new: the pews and the front of the gallery are well carved, but the most notable features are the carved oak cornice round the nave walls and the panelled wall of the south transept. Much of this woodwork came from the old manor-house which had fallen into disrepair and which was finally demolished when Lord Bathurst formed the great park through which we have walked. Even Pope did not see eye to eye with his Lordship in this instance—

> "All vast possessions (just the same the case
> Whether you call them villa, park or chase)
> Alas, my Bathurst, what will they avail?
> Join Cotswold hills to Sapperton's fair dale;
> Link towns to towns with avenues of oak
> Enclose whole downs with walls: 'tis all a joke!
> Inexorable death shall level all,
> And trees and stones and farmer fall."

Two conspicuous monuments in the church commemorate former owners of the manor. In the north transept is an elaborate affair of colour and carving in memory of Sir Henry Poole and his wife, with effigies also of their family: a grandiose affair, perhaps, but in accordance with the fashion of the period in which it was erected, and of extraordinary interest for the care with which features and costumes are portrayed. On the east wall of the south transept is the monument of Sir Robert Atkyns, historian of Gloucestershire. He inherited the manor-house from his father, but continued to live at Pinbury Park, a mile or two higher up the valley, until his death in 1711. Note also the fifteenth-century octagonal font and the carved Jacobean Communion Table.

John Masefield lived at Sapperton for some years. So did Sir Stafford Cripps, who is buried in the churchyard.

From Sapperton a lane dips steeply down to the foot of the valley, crossing the now derelict **Severn and Thames Canal** near the entrance to the tunnel, $2\frac{1}{2}$ miles long, which carried its waters under the Cotswolds. Up to the right we climb through beech-woods, presently coming to a lane on the right leading to **Edge-worth**. On the right are the gates and lodge of Edgeworth Manor. After passing the gates turn down to the right. With lovely views through the wooded valley, the public road leads to the church in an idyllic position on a projecting spur of the hillside, so sheltered with tall trees that one realizes with astonishment that the sun can penetrate to the sundial over the church porch. Notwithstanding the old door and pew-ends, the roof and the modern rood-loft in the church, one's principal memory of Edgeworth is mainly concerned with trees; the box hedges in the churchyard looking like huge billowy cushions. Even so, the church is of almost unspoiled Norman architecture.

A mile farther along the brow of the Frome Valley is **Miserden.** The name is the modern version of Musard, the family who held it in the twelfth and thirteenth centuries. In Miserden Church is a very fine monument in the south choir aisle to Sir William Sandys (1640), his wife and children. There is a Saxon doorway and arch, a Norman font and several architecturally interesting details. The Rectory adjoining dates back to 1605 and has recently been restored as the parsonage house.

East of Miserden, across the valley, is **Winstone,** a straggly village whose church is tucked away among farmyards as though fearful that modern innovations will invade its privacy and sweep away the many memorials of the church which the Normans built on this spot. Although much restored in 1876, the little church with its saddle-back tower has retained the Norman south doorway and an earlier blocked north doorway and chancel arch which may be Saxon. At the south entrance is the base of a fourteenth-century churchyard cross. Winstone is a mile away from the Akeman Street, and little of the traffic hurrying along between Cirencester and Gloucester has time to turn aside.

It is noticeable how groups of villages alongside a river perpetuate their situation in their names. The Coln and Ampney villages are near examples, and so we realize that the Duntisbournes take the first part of their names from their situation in the valley of the little Dun. **Duntisbourne Leer** as a name is more understandable when we recall that of old it belonged to the abbey of Lire, in Normandy. **Duntisbourne Abbots**—formerly a possession of Gloucester—has a church with a large tower and an attractive Norman font: more interesting is that at **Duntisbourne Rous** (named after the Rous family), and more typically Cotswold is the hamlet in the way its cottages are gathered together down by the river. The church is built on such a slope that there is a crypt below the chancel—rare in a building of so small a size. The church, in fact, seems to progress in stages from east to west: the chancel, the nave, and finally the low saddleback tower which so admirably suits the general lines of the building. There is much Saxon and Norman work within and without, and altogether it can be classed with those lovable little buildings where one can linger and from which one brings away lasting memories.

Of all the churches beside the Dun, however, that at—

## Daglingworth

is outstanding for its Saxon and Norman work, chief of which are the three stone panels which Saxon masons carved to represent The Crucifixion, Christ Enthroned, and St. Peter.

These stones were found built into the jambs of the chancel arch when the chancel and sanctuary were rebuilt 1845–50. They had been inserted with their carved faces inward, so that from Norman times until last century no one had seen them. A fourth carving, another representation of the Crucifixion, can be seen on the outside of the church above the east window.

Such a transplanting is, however, in accordance with the building: a small Norman window which formerly lit the nave was removed to

131

Barnsley (*see* p. 136). The Norman altar now at the east end of Daglingworth Church was originally in a priest's chamber in the vanished tower. The three arches which face us as we enter the church are no older than the 1845 "restoration" when, in addition to the rebuilding of the chancel, the north aisle was added.

At Daglingworth is a very fine example of the old circular dovecot furnished inside with a revolving ladder to enable the nesting-holes to be reached. The ladder is supported on two horizontal beams which in turn stretch like arms from a central revolving pillar. There are upwards of 500 nesting-holes in the wall.

# THE CHURN VALLEY

Although the Ordnance Map marks the **Source of the River Thames** at Thames Head Bridge, on the Fosse Way 3 miles south-west of Cirencester, the fact that this source is frequently dry lends support to the contention that the true source of the Thames is at the Seven Springs, near Coberley, some 10 miles north of Cirencester. In this case the Churn might be renamed the Thames or Isis; but under any name it provides a very interesting and enjoyable excursion. Past **Baunton,** with a church containing a well-preserved life-size fifteenth-century wall painting of St. Christopher, we come from Cirencester to **Bagendon,** nestling among trees in a little side-valley: a place of grey stone roofs and with a church that has some surprisingly good glass in its windows, both old and new.

## North Cerney

again is a pretty village but it is its church that mostly attracts visitors.

Largely rebuilt about 1470 following a fire, it still retains features from the original Norman church; the lower part of the tower, the early Norman south doorway, and the fine late Norman chancel arch. There is a fifteenth-century stone pulpit, beautifully carved, and the windows of both transepts show fifteenth-century stained glass. Above the modern rood-loft is a Cotswold feature, a window now blocked above the chancel arch. In 1959 an interesting find was a carved twelfth-century gravestone, used in repair after the fire as a lintel over the south window of the tower which, originally square-topped, was then reduced to its present "saddle-back" form. At the same time there came to light a piece of Saxon carving of the Crucifixion not unlike one of the Daglingworth panels. This evidence of a pre-Norman church has been inserted into the splay of a window on the south side of the Chancel. Note the lovely and well-restored fourteenth-century cross and the delightful rectory.

**Rendcombe** is delightfully situated overlooking the Churn Valley. The church was rebuilt early in the sixteenth century by that John Tame who rebuilt Fairford Church. It contains a fine chancel screen, some ancient glass and a circular Norman font depicting the apostles, which is beautiful and interesting.

For some miles Rendcombe Park borders the Churn and our road as they come down from **Colesbourne,** with another park that is famous for its trees and its memories of Henry Elwes, co-author of *The Trees of Britain*. For **Elkstone,** *see* p. 66.

Still following the valley of the Churn, we next arrive at **Cowley** with its fine manor-house built in 1674. The grounds surrounding the house are watered by a lovely chain of lakes. The little church of Norman origin contains many features of interest although the building was drastically restored in 1872.

Less than a mile away is—

## Coberley

where Dick Whittington lived for a time at the now-vanished Coberley Hall. This hall, which adjoined the church, was long the home of the Berkeleys, and Sir Thomas Berkeley who fought at Crecy was the first husband of Lady Joan, who, after his death in 1350, married Sir William Whittington and became mother of Richard Whittington of Pauntley in 1359. After his father's death, Dick and his twice-widowed mother often visited Coberley. Later he thrice became Lord Mayor of London.

Coberley Hall was pulled down in the latter half of the eighteenth century, but for evidence of those earlier times it is only necessary to go to the church and look at the tombs of the Berkeleys in the south

133

chapel: that of Sir Thomas de Berkeley (who endowed and built the south chapel in 1340) and Lady Joan whose tomb lies close beside. Both these tombs were moved from the sanctuary when the church was restored in 1870, but remaining in the sanctuary is a heart-burial monument—the only example of its kind in the Cotswolds. This monument is thought to represent Sir Giles de Berkeley, father of Sir Thomas, who died and was buried at Little Malvern in 1295 but whose heart was brought home to Coberley for burial. Directly outside the church, against the south boundary wall, is buried Sir Giles' favourite charger, Lombard.

Tradition says that Charles I stayed at the old Manor-house and that his son stayed at the Rectory (the present Rectory was built on the site of the old one in 1814). Few were aware how illustrious a guest the roof sheltered that night for Charles was on his adventurous journey from Worcester's fatal field and was disguised as a manservant.

So to the **Seven Springs,** with its inscribed plate:

HIC TUUS
O TAMESINE PATER
SEPTEMGEMINUS FONS

Here, in fact, is the highest source of the Thames: tree-shaded and by-passed by a new road, it provides a quiet resting place for travellers. A truly humble start for such a great river as the Thames. Who would think that the waters of this small stream, that commences with the name Churn as it trickles through Coberley, Cowley and Colesbourne, could ever pass beneath the bridges of the great metropolis? Those whose lot it is to be more familiar with the Pool of London than with this little pool among the Cotswolds can take away many pleasant memories of sunny days at Coberley.

# THE AMPNEYS

Between 2 and 5 miles eastward from Cirencester on the Fairford road are three villages taking the first part of their names from the Ampney stream, which adds its mite to the Thames near Cricklade. Of the three, the nearest to Cirencester is **Ampney Crucis,** an oasis of cottages standing in gay gardens and ripe orchards and with a picturesque water-mill and fine upstanding church. So tucked away among trees is it as to be easily overlooked by those using the main road, but it is well worth turning aside to visit.

At the southern entrance to the churchyard is a very ancient cross on a worn stone base, and to the south of the church is a very fine fifteenth-century cross. The name of the village, however, has no relation to these crosses, for the church is dedicated to the Holy Cross and in Domesday is referred to as the church of Omenie Holy Rood.

Inside, the church is notable for its Norman chancel arch with bold chevron work, and the blocked doorway in the north wall: possibly Saxon, certainly not later than Norman.

Behind the pulpit note the woodwork of the rood-loft doorway; the bricked-up opening above it led to the loft itself. In the north transept is the tomb of George Lloyde, one-time Lord of the Manor. The north transept bears traces of mural painting: all that is left of the many paintings with which the building was once decorated.

A mile or so east of Ampney Crucis the church of **Ampney St. Mary** stands apart from the village.

Approaching from the road one's attention is caught by the tympanum over the blocked north doorway, carved with a double-headed serpent, a griffin and another monster, the whole group "telling a tale that was perhaps more understood 800 years ago". The nave walls bear numerous traces of early painting and just east of the narrow chancel arch is a remnant of the old stone screen. The large holes in the wall on either side of the arch probably held the ends of beams supporting the rood-loft. Just west of the south porch is a window consisting of two lights carved from a single block of stone, possibly by Norman masons.

The most interesting feature of the church, however, is the wall paintings, concerning which Mr. L. W. Barnard remarks, in a little handbook obtainable from the verger:

"The walls of the Church had been covered with a colour wash, but underneath were frescoes of an extremely interesting nature. Evidently in the thirteenth century a system of decoration had been carried out consisting chiefly of lines representing masonry and floral patterns, which though probably very fine at the time was not sufficiently elaborate and pictorial, for within a few years it seems that the whole church was redecorated, this time with a bold set of pictures, of which we now have a few good fragments—notably a large-size Crucifixion on the south wall close to the rood beam, and a curious figure seated among wheels and having a circular shaft projecting from his eye. It has been suggested that this might represent the parable of the beam, but it does not seem very clear. Then there are the Five Wise Virgins with their lamps alight, apparently going to a crowned figure (very much mutilated) with minstrels playing different musical instruments.

"On the north wall are some more scraps of paintings, a sky scene studded with stars and having crowned faces appeaïing over an altar with Norman zigzag ornaments. This picture might be taken from the book of Revelation, but, like the other picture, it is rather difficult to be quite sure as to the meaning.

"Hidden behind the pulpit is a figure robed in blue and green, but evidently before it was whitewashed over someone had smashed up the head and face. The figure might represent a bishop as it holds a staff, otherwise both from the colouring and the position one would expect it to represent the Virgin."

The third Ampney, **Ampney St. Peter,** lies on the main Cirencester—Fairford road.

About 4 miles south-east is **Down Ampney,** famous as the birthplace of Ralph Vaughan Williams, and one of his hymn tunes bears its name.

A mile or two northward and almost midway between Cirencester and Bibury (*see* p. 40), **Barnsley** is utterly unlike its great northern namesake, and the many farm buildings give a refreshed significance to the name. With its rows of dormer-windowed cottages set behind gay little gardens that are contained in walls just like huge flower-boxes, it is one of the prettiest of villages. A church has stood here since Norman times: the north doorway and the shafts of the chancel arch remain, and a number of quaint corbel heads look down on the organ. The church was restored in 1848 when all traces of its previous Georgian remodelling were removed. The windows are nineteenth-century except for that moved here from Daglingworth.

Barnsley Park was built for Henry Perrot, a nephew by marriage of the Duke of Chandos, in 1720, and contains outstanding stucco decoration. The old rectory, now known as Barnsley House, was built in 1697. In the garden is a Gothic summer house and an Adam temple moved from Fairford in 1962.

# Stroud and Neighbourhood

## Stroud

**Access.**—Frequent buses and coaches from and to Gloucester, Cheltenham, Cirencester, Painswick, etc. *Station* on Western Region main line London to Cheltenham, *via* Swindon.

**Art Gallery.**—Exhibitions at George Room Gallery, daily, free.

**Boating** on the Ship Canal at Frampton-on-Severn or on the Severn at Framilode.

**Bowls.**—Six Cumberland turf rinks in Stratford Park; and in Victoria Park.

**Distances.**—Bath, 28 miles; Cirencester, 12; Gloucester, 9; Cheltenham, 13; London, 102.

**Early Closing.**—Thursday

**Festival.**—Annually in mid-October, a Festival of Drama and of the Arts.

**Gliding.**—Clubs at Nympsfield and Aston Down.

**Golf.**—*Minchinhampton Golf Club*; an 18-hole course on Minchinhampton Common. The hazards consist partly of artificial bunkers and partly of quarries and prehistoric entrenchments. The views are glorious.

The links at Painswick and on Stinchcombe Hill (p. 145) are within easy reach.

**Hotels.**—*See* p. 12.

**Population.**—19,600.

**Putting Green** in Stratford Park.

**Swimming.**—A splendid modern pool in Stratford Park, with a special bath for children. The amenities include terraces for spectators, a café, and sunbathing terraces.

**Tennis.**—Public courts in Stratford Park.

In medieval times the famous Cotswold wool was mainly exported *via* the "Staple" at Calais, for manufacture abroad. In the reigns of Edward II and III, the importation of cloth from abroad was prohibited, and cloth manufacture increased apace, until by Tudor times the export of cloth had completely replaced that of wool.

Stroud and its neighbourhood became increasingly devoted to the manufacture of broadcloth, the River Frome and its tributaries providing the necessary water supply for fulling mills and for dyeing processes. Fine West of England cloth is still manufactured at Stroud, but a variety of other industries have established themselves, particularly in plastics.

The town is not unattractive, with its steep narrow streets. Despite its great antiquity, it is now primarily a shopping and business centre for the surrounding rural districts, and not a show town for tourists. Stroud is nevertheless an admirable centre from which to see the south-west Cotswolds. Cheltenham, Cirencester, and Gloucester are within easy reach, and 1,500 acres of commons and open spaces surround the town.

The **Old Town Hall**, in Church Street, still preserves some of its sixteenth-century features, and there are some old cottages of interest near by. Though not rich in historical buildings, Stroud is well provided with open spaces. On the Gloucester road is the beautiful and extensive **Stratford Park**, which has gardens, swimming pool, and other facilities for sport. Nearer to the centre of the town are the well-kept **Bank Gardens** and **Park Gardens**, and at Ebley, a mile to the west, is **Victory Park**. From many parts of the town one can look southward across the valley of the Frome to **Rodborough Fort** (p. 142). The **Museum**, in Lansdown, has many exhibits relating to industrial archaeology.

From Stroud to Sapperton (p. 129)—half-way to Cirencester—lies the "**Golden Valley**" of the Frome. Though peaceful enough today, except when its echoes are awakened by a passing train, this valley was once busy with industry and an incessant stream of barges passed along the Thames and Severn Canal, all laden with bales of cloth or coal. But the canal is disused, the locks are

broken and parts of the Sapperton tunnel have fallen in.

On the high ground to the north of the valley, and easily reached by road from Stroud, is **Bisley**, a place of some significance in English church history, for a century ago its vicar was Thomas Keble, younger brother of John Keble.

Bisley Church has interests dating much earlier than the time of Keble. The font is an exceptionally fine example of Norman work, and in various parts of the building are evidences that at one time the neighbourhood boasted some clever carvers both in wood and stone: note, for example, the little figures helping to uphold the roof. But most interesting of all is the unique thirteenth-century Well Head, which contained the poor soul's light, in the churchyard.

Just below the church is a spot known as the **Seven Springs** not, of course, to be confused with the Seven Springs nearer Coberley (*see* p. 134). From a short piece of wall five springs spurt out from little recesses which have aptly been compared to piscinae, and two other springs emerge from spouts. Here on Ascension Day is held the ancient ceremony of "well dressing".

At **Lypiatt Park,** a little to the west, the Gunpowder Plot conspirators are known to have met. **Over Court,** adjoining Bisley Church, is a fine mansion that was once the property of Elizabeth I, who is reported to have stayed here.

To the north-west of Bisley lies the steep **Slad Valley,** once a centre of cloth making. From Stroud the B4070 winds and twists up the valley, with grand beech woods on the left and down below on the right the little stream and **Slad** village.

Farther up the valley is **Bull's Cross,** a kind of saddle between the Slad and the Painswick Valleys from which one has one of the best views of Painswick. From this point one may ascend to the small and precipitous village of **Sheepscombe,** whose name recalls the former predominant feature of the Cotswold scene.

## Painswick

Access.—Bus connection with trains at Stroud and Gloucester. Buses and coaches from and to Cheltenham, Cirencester, Stroud, Malmesbury and Gloucester.
Distances.—Cheltenham, 10 miles; Gloucester, 6; Stroud, 4.
Early Closing.—Saturday.
Golf Course on the slopes of Kimsbury Hill—a very sporting 18-hole course among exhilarating surroundings.
Hotels.—*See* p. 11.
Licensing Hours.—10–2.30, 6–10.30; Sundays, 12–2, 7–10.30.

Painswick, on the main road from Cheltenham to Stroud, has been called "Queen of the Cotswolds". Drawings and photographs innumerable have made the clipped yews of the place familiar throughout the land. The yews are easy marks, but it must not be thought that all Painswick springs so easily to the surface. In quite a short walk through apparently quite ordinary streets one encounters little scenes which baffle one by the almost startling air of quiet assurance with which they face the world. This air is not in any obvious way dependent upon architecture or site or surroundings, or even on one's train of thought, but seems to emanate as from an inner consciousness: one receives an overwhelming impression that here is a spot which has witnessed happiness and tragedy and which is no longer in the heyday of youth, but which is still intensely strong and confident and unruffled by the clashes and clangours of these times. It is a sensation common, doubtless, to many who have explored the Cotswolds, but in few places is the impression so vivid.

Painswick has seen both happiness and tragedy. Here Ann Boleyn spent two happy days with Henry VIII but a year before tragedy befell her on Tower Hill. Here, too, came Charles I in 1643, full of hopes for the capture of Gloucester—and here he came again a month later, his hopes dashed. And lest it be thought that Painswick's experience of tragedy is purely of a vicarious nature, let us recall that Sir Anthony Kingston (whose father had been Anne Boleyn's jailer) was lord of the manor, a sinister and ruthless individual who built a prison in Painswick, and a gallows at Sheepscombe.

From such memories it is a relief to turn to the famous bowling green of the *Falcon Hotel* and the clipped yews of the churchyard, the latter formerly the "place of resort for the ladies and polite inhabitants of the town in fine weather". There are more than 99 yews, some over 200 years old, and their clipping is a task of considerable length. There is no connection between this event and the present day "Clipping" procession held every September, when the parishioners join hands and encircle or "clip" their church. ("clippen" = to embrace.)

The picturesque lychgate (A.D. 1900) at the south-west corner of the churchyard incorporates much timber from the old belfry. The inscriptions on the structure are unusual; so, too, are the spectacle-type iron stocks at the south-east corner of the churchyard.

### Painswick Church

occupies the site of a building dating from Norman times, though it is principally early fifteenth-century work—a date significant to those who know their Cotswolds, for this was the heyday of the wool trade, when the wealthy merchants were proud to build and adorn their churches. The church of Painswick has not escaped disaster, however, for after Charles's failure to capture Gloucester some of the Parliamentary troops took refuge in it from Sir Wm. Vavasour, the Royalist commander, and damage was done by his "firing the doores and casting in hand-grenades". In 1883 the spire was struck by lightning and crashed through the roof into the church.

Painswick Church is a beautiful building, but even more beautiful are a sixteenth-century stone house known as **The Court House** (*Thurs. 2–5*), and **Castle Hale,** a seventeenth-century house on the site of the ancient manorhouse of Payn Fitz John: its history is enshrined in Dr. St. Clair Baddeley's *Cotteswold Manor.*

Painswick stands on a tongue of high land flowing down from **Painswick Beacon** (922 feet), a splendid view-point and the site of the Golf Links. Here too are the remains of a triangular hill-fort known as *Kimsbury Camp*, for which reason the hill is frequently referred to as **Kimsbury Hill.**

The best view-point in the vicinity, however, is **Haresfield Beacon,** 2 miles south-west and reached by way of secluded little **Pitchcombe.** Over 700 feet above the sea, and now happily in the care of the National Trust, Haresfield Beacon is one of the finest of the many fine view-points along this western edge of the Cotswolds. On the crest of the Beacon a view indicator assists identification of principal points. Almost at one's feet lies Gloucester; to the south-west the Severn can be followed in an ever-broadening band of silver, and the hills beyond the Forest of Dean lose themselves in range after range of Welsh mountains.

Such an outpost would obviously have been of importance in ancient days, and the Romans had a large camp here. In 1837 no fewer than 3,000 Roman coins, minted fifteen hundred years before, were discovered. Down in the village is a mound thought to have been raised by the Danes or Saxons, and there is also a monument commemorating the siege of Gloucester in 1643.

**Haresfield Church** was built by the Normans. Among its unusual features is the double chancel, though it has been suggested that the eastern part was originally a Lady Chapel. In the north wall of the chancel are two effigies (originally there were three) of which one, showing a lady in a wimple, dates from 1320.

Dryden wrote the epitaph over the grave, at Haresfield, of eleven-year-old John Rogers—

> "Knowing Heaven his home, to shun delay
> He leap'd o'er age and took the shortest way."

A much rarer inscription is to be seen in the south porch of the church at **Brookthorpe**, a couple of miles nearer Gloucester. It is a chronogram, a date being hidden in the words:

TER *D*ANO *I*AN*I* *L*ABENS RE*X* SO*L*E *C*A*D*ENTE
*CAROLV*S E*XVTV*S SO*LI*O S*C*EPTRO*QV*E SE*CV*RE

## THE SOUTHERN ENVIRONS OF STROUD

To the south of the Golden Valley, and between it and the valley in which is Nailsworth, is a tongue of high land bearing two fine commons—those of Rodborough and of Minchinhampton. **Rodborough Fort,** at the northern end of Rodborough Common, is a comparatively modern castellated mansion, and has no military significance. It is, however, a very familiar landmark to all who explore the district, and the views from its vicinity are wonderful. South of **Rodborough Common,** and looking down into the Nailsworth Valley, is the picturesque village of **Amberley,** notable for the fact that Mrs. Craik wrote part of *John Halifax, Gentleman,* while staying at Rose Cottage. Amberley is the "Enderley" of the novel and the Common is "Enderley Flat".

Both Rodborough Common, and the more extensive **Minchinhampton Common** that adjoins it, are now National Trust property. A signpost where six roads meet on Minchinhampton Common is marked "Tom Long's Post", and marks a spot where highwaymen were buried.

## Minchinhampton

is better known for its golf links (*see* p. 137), laid out on the glorious common, than as a seat of industry, but time was when it was a very busy centre of cloth-making. The **Market House**, dating from 1698, and supported on pillars, is a picturesque feature. But the most remarkable building in the town is **Holy Trinity Church,** crowned by something that can best be described as a truncated steeple trimmed with pinnacles, the latter having been added during a Victorian restoration. Among the brasses in the church is one commemorating James Bradley, Astronomer-Royal in 1742 and the discoverer of the aberration of fixed stars. Other brasses are in the north-west corner of the church. The beautiful south transept was built in 1382 by that Robert de la Bere who, with his wife, lies in effigy beneath the south window.

On the outskirts of Minchinhampton is the fine park of **Gatcombe,** built in 1770 by "Mr. Sheppard, an eminent clothier", and later the home of David Ricardo, the famous political economist. It is now owned by Lord Butler (R. A. Butler).

The Sheppards also at one time owned the manor of **Avening,** a pretty village situated alongside the Avening brook. Avening Church still retains many of its Norman features, but there

143

are good examples of the work of later periods. In view of the references already made to the Sheppard family, it is worth noting that there is a monument in the north transept to Henry Brydges, fourth son of John, Lord Chandos. "This Henry Brydges," says Edward Hutton, "was a queer character. In his youthful days he lived the life of a freebooter 'indulging in deeds of lawlessness surpassing powers of belief', and eventually succeeded in his greatest coup by marrying the eldest daughter of the 'eminent clothier', Samuel Sheppard. After that triumph he settled down here—his father-in-law was lord of the manor—and here he lies."

From Avening one could return to Stroud by way of **Nailsworth** (pop. 4,240) a small town in a delightful position at the foot of a steep valley. Here, as at Stroud, some cloth is still manufactured, but it has in recent years become a residential retreat, with happily-placed houses sprinkled over the hill-slopes. "Nailsworth Ladder" with its formidable gradient (in places nearly 1 in 2) and its treacherous surface, is well known as a scene of motor cycle trials. Southward a pretty road goes to **Horsley,** passing on the way some extensive fish hatcheries: westward one could climb the hill track to 700 feet to **Nympsfield,** whence one looks out over mile upon mile of the Severn Valley, with the winding course of the river like a broad band of silver among the green meadows and beyond it the hills of the Forest of Dean. Gliding is popular here (Bristol Gliding Club).

South of Nympsfield, near the B4058 from Nailsworth to Dursley, is the delightful hamlet of **Owlpen,** with its Tudor manor-house (*Friday afternoons, June and July*), church, mill, and court-house.

From Owlpen's lovely manor-house the lane rises steeply to **Uley,** sprinkled along the western side of the Cam Valley—a village of calm and of exquisite views, though these qualities are even more keenly apparent from the great Barrow—**Hetty Pegler's Tump**—on the hill-top above the village, and after Belas Knap the finest barrow in the Cotswold. Today it is merely a great earthen mound, and except to archaeologists there is small attraction in exploring the interior, but this was the burial-place of men who lived here at about the time Stonehenge was being built, and the beauty of the situation is apparent. Thirty skeletons were found in the barrow when it was opened last century.

From the Camp, nearly 800 feet above the sea, we look down on to Cam Long Down and Downham Hill, rising like islands from the green fields, and between them see **Dursley**, hardly 2 miles distant but much more happily approached by way of **Whiteway Hill,** turning off the road to Wotton-under-Edge about 3 miles north of that town. Coming thus we have a splendid run down through woods which suddenly part on the right to show an exquisite picture framed by Downham Hill and Cam Long Down on the right and **Stinchcombe Hill** on the left, with **Dursley** in the foreground and beyond it the familiar but never satiating view of the Severn plain backed by the Forest of Dean Hills.

Down in the valley is Slimbridge, where Peter Scott has established the Wildfowl Trust (*Admission charge*) to promote research.


## Dursley

Once a market town and cloth-making centre, Dursley has developed during the present century into a busy manufacturing area, with a population of about 5,000, many of whom are employed in agricultural and general engineering works.

This industrial development has modified the former picturesque aspect of the town. The old **Market Hall,** supported on pillars and with arches, bell turret and wind-vane, dates from 1738. There are old houses near the church, at Broadwell and in several of the streets. The church, largely a fifteenth-century building with nineteenth-century restoration work, has a fine carved roof and a fourteenth-century font.

Hanging woods above the town provide pleasant walks.

On **Stinchcombe Hill,** above Dursley, is a splendid 18-hole golf course with fine views over the Severn estuary.

To return to Stroud from Dursley let us take the attractive

road below the Edge, and from which we can better appreciate the suddenness with which the Cotswolds fall to the plain on this side. It is well worth diverging to **Frocester** for the sake of its fine sixteenth-century manor-house with its lovely gateway, wherein Queen Elizabeth I stayed, and the thirteenth-century tithe-barn, measuring 184 feet by 30 feet and believed to be the largest in England. The building appeals not solely on account of its size and its magnificent roof, but for the dignity and grace of style designed to harmonize with its surroundings.

Smaller but hardly less striking is the tithe-barn at neighbouring **Leonard Stanley**, a pleasant village, named after the Priory of St. Leonard, some buildings of which remain, the most important being the church with its massive tower. It is a fine cruciform building without aisles, entirely Norman, except for some of the windows, the porch, and a very fine wagon-roof, all the work of the fourteenth and fifteenth centuries. There are also some very interesting carvings in stone. An unusual feature is the little window lighting the stairway to the rood-loft: part of the rood-beam itself is now in the north transept. Near the west end of the church are the remains of a Saxon Parish Church, dedicated to St. Swithin, Bishop of Winchester (*died* 962).

Neighbouring the Stanley which belonged to the Priory of St. Leonard is the Stanley which was of the King. It lies at the foot of Selsley Hill (689 feet), rising like a bastion before the Edge just west of **Woodchester,** a name well known to those interested in Roman remains, for here was discovered one of the finest Roman villas in the land. Many of the treasures found when the remains were examined are now to be seen in Gloucester Museum, but in the old churchyard is a very fine tessellated pavement, 12 yards each way and having in its centre a beautifully wrought representation of Orpheus. In order to protect it, the pavement has been covered over again and is uncovered only on occasions.

Woodchester is the site of a Franciscan Convent and a Dominican Priory: the latter is regarded as the mother church of the present Dominican Order in England, having been the first to be established here since the Reformation.

# The Southern Cotswolds

## Bath to Stroud

The southernmost range of the Cotswolds is a strip of high land about 25 miles from north to south, narrowing in places to a width of hardly more than 2 miles, and never more than 10 miles from east to west. Except in places it is less typically Cotswold than any other part of the range. The Edges have little of the majesty that one finds at Stanway and the contours have not the beauty of the downs between Stow and Broadway, while the architecture is more and more definitely under the influence of Bath.

The main road runs along the top of the ridge all the way, being crossed by innumerable roads running east and west across the hills. As the places of interest are so few miles distant from each other, we shall take the main road as the backbone of our route, so to speak, and make excursions either side.

The route from Bath leaves the London road at the fork about a mile from the Abbey and climbs past Swainswick and the historic hill of Solsbury. A mile or so farther a fork road on the right leads to **Cold Ashton** with a good view of the charming manor-house, and thence the route is through **Marshfield,** an interesting village with some noteworthy buildings. A few miles farther a left-hand turn leads towards Castle Combe (12 miles from Bath), which is reached finally by turning sharply back to the left at a road junction at the end of a beech wood.

## Castle Combe

The attractions of this delightful village have been thus aptly summed up by Mr. Edward Hutton (*Highways and Byways in Wilts*): "In its character it belongs not to Wilts at all, but to the west country, and in its own way it is as unique as Clovelly. It lies in the bottom and climbs a little way up the hill-side and is dominated wholly by the great wooded hill upon which the Norman Castle which names it stood of old. . . . But long before

147

the Dunstanvilles built this castle here, Castle Combe existed, as the prehistoric earthworks on the castle hill witness."

The church tower is very fine, but unfortunately the church was rebuilt during last century, and, except for the chancel arch and one or two carefully preserved features, is of comparatively little interest. The gem of the village is the fine market-cross, delightful to look at or to loiter in on a hot sunny day. The whole village, however, is a place in which to linger and to which to return—flower-covered cottages and delightful old houses making up a picture that would be difficult to match.

From Castle Combe we make a north-westerly way back to the Stroud road just above **Old Sodbury,** set on the hillside and with grand views over the plain. The church was originally Norman, but is now principally interesting for the two effigies in the north transept: one of stone, the other of wood and said to represent Philip le Gros (1270). Warriors earlier than these knew these hills, however, for above the village is a very extensive British encampment within which a Roman camp was subsequently built. The spot is worth visiting whether one is archaeologically minded or merely seeking a good view-point: on a clear day the outlook is magnificent.

## Chipping Sodbury

The most southerly of three Cotswold Chippings, Chipping Sodbury has an exceptionally wide main street which seems to confirm the aptness of the name, for Chipping here as elsewhere meant "market". Its buildings in the main street are all built of stone. Although much of the surrounding district is still rural, there has been a marked increase of industries in the last twenty years: quarries, engineering works, saw mills and flour mills provide employment for many of the inhabitants. New housing estates are spreading rapidly, particularly in the direction of Bristol. A Mop fair is held twice yearly.

Chipping Sodbury **Church** is an imposing building with a lofty west tower. It was originally the Chapel of Ease to Old Sodbury Church and dates mainly from the fifteenth century. Among the many interesting things in the church is the pulpit, which was hidden for centuries by a three-decker but revealed by G. E. Street when restoring

148

the church in 1869. It is unusual in the way in which it is built against the easternmost pier of the nave and entered by a doorway through the pier, and very beautiful in the detail of its design. Another unusual architectural feature found here is the corbels supporting the thirteenth-century chancel arch; instead of the customary head or leaf one finds short lengths of stone carved so that they resemble nothing so much as barley sugar. Other items of interest are the font, piscina and the old rood-loft stairs.

A mile west of Chipping Sodbury is **Yate,** a fascinating place with a church notable for its tower and its medieval wall-paintings, including a St. Christopher. Between nave and aisle is a curious double pillar; several of the windows have exceptionally good glass and in the south chapel is a splendid brass to Alexander Staples, showing also his two wives and eleven children.

Two miles north of the village is **Yate Court,** a rebuilding of an earlier house by the Berkeleys, when they were dispossessed of Berkeley Castle.

From Yate Court we can make a direct way back to the hills or return through the two Sodburys, but before ascending it is worth while skirting the edge as far as **Hawkesbury,** where the hill is crowned by a lofty tower commemorating Lord E. H. Somerset (d. 1842). Hawkesbury Church dates from Saxon times, and can show also some good Norman work, but the building as a whole has been so restored and reconstructed that one is never quite sure what is old and what new. An unusual feature for a church is its possession of three fireplaces.

In the porch is a quaintly worded notice—

> It is Desired that
> All Persons that come to
> This Church would be careful
> to leave their Dogs at home and
> that the Women would not walk
> in with their Pattens on.

South-east of Hawkesbury is **Badminton Park,** for three centuries the home of the noble family of Beaufort. The park is 10 miles round and is celebrated for its trees. The house is approached from Great Badminton and is *open to the public on Wednesday afternoons from May to the first Wednesday in September*. It is a fine example of the Palladian style and contains a valuable collection of paintings in the Italian, Dutch and

English Schools together with carving and furniture of great interest. For some years Badminton has been internationally famous for the Three Day Event Horse Trials.

From the main road to Cirencester a splendid view of Worcester Lodge can be obtained. Situated at the north end of the Park this archway was designed by William Kent and is considered to be one of his best works.

From Hawkesbury a minor road leads westward to **Wickwar** where there is a fifteenth-century church having an interesting roof and, near by, a seventeenth-century grammar school and a pack horse bridge. North of Wickwar is **Charfield,** with its fourteenth-century church standing deserted away from the village and the modern church erected a mile to the south.

Beyond Charfield is **Tortworth,** with a celebrated Spanish chestnut tree probably a thousand years old and measuring nearly 60 feet round. Though its great trunk has been aptly described as "a fantastic mass", the tree is still vigorously alive and a splendid sight it makes.

Tortworth Church was rebuilt, with the exception of the tower, in 1872, but it has a thirteenth-century font and two fine monuments to the Throckmortons dated respectively 1568 and 1607.

The former Tortworth Court is now a prison establishment.

But it is time we returned to the hills, taking the road through **Kingswood,** at one time the seat of a prosperous Abbey of Cistercians, of which the fifteenth-century gate-house is almost the sole remnant.


## Wotton-under-Edge

Access.—By bus or coach from Bristol (20 miles), Gloucester (18), and Stroud (12).
Banks.—*Lloyds, National Westminster, Midland.*
Early Closing.—Wednesday.
Fishing.—Good sport (coarse fish and some trout) in Tortworth Lakes.
Golf at Stinchcombe (*see* p. 145) and Minchinhampton (p. 143).
Hotels.—*See* p. 12.
Population.—4,318.

The name is not quite accurately descriptive, for it suggests overhanging cliffs, whereas the town is set out on a spur of high ground, and one of the joys of the main street (Londoners note with pleasure that the lower part is named Ludgate Hill) are the views of woods and smooth green slopes on the far side of the valley. The predominant feature of this High Street is the ancient **Tolsey,** its tiled pyramidal roof crowned by a cupola supporting a weather vane in the form of a dragon.

Market Street, beside the Tolsey, leads to the open place formerly used as the market-place and still known as **The Chipping.** In Long Street is the picturesque seventeenth-century Berkeley House, and the town has many other delightful groups, notably the steeply-gabled almshouses in Church Street (1634).

Noted residents were Isaac Pitman, who while schoolmaster here a century ago taught shorthand and wrote his *Stenographic Sound Hand,* the precursor of a long line of famous manuals; and Edward Jenner, the discoverer of vaccination, who was educated at the **Grammar School**—one of the earliest scholastic foundations in England, dating from 1384.

**St. Mary's Church** is notable for its lofty pinnacled tower, the grey stone of which shows up very beautifully against the distant woods. The interior of the building is light and spacious and there are some fine old brasses. The organ is of interest as having originally been given by George I to the church of St. Martin-in-the-Fields, London (Buckingham Palace is within the parish of St. Martin's). At the end of the north aisle is a memorial to Thomas, 10th Lord Berkeley (1352–1417), and his wife, with two good brasses, he with a lion at his feet, she with a dog. Let in the floor of the tower is a stone formerly over the tomb of Richard of Wotton, founder and first rector of the church (1320). Unfortunately the brass has been torn off, but the matrix remains.

An unusual feature of the church is the little St. Katharine's Chapel, opening off the north aisle.

The various monuments in the church will confirm what the observant visitor has already surmised, that in past days Wotton was a busy centre of cloth-weaving: indeed, the name is held to be derived from "Wool-town". There are no looms in Wotton today, but three large mills at the neighbouring village of **Kingswood** (*see* p. 150) manufacture elastic fabrics and may in a sense be held to carry on the tradition.

Of the country around Wotton it is impossible to speak too highly, for it is broken up into little wooded combes which are a delight to explore, and as one makes one's way about the higher ground there are constant surprises in the extent of the views—not merely westward over the Severn plain to the Forest of Dean, but far to the south and east. About 3 miles north of the town, above **North Nibley,** is a monument commemorating William Tyndale, translator of the Bible: the tradition that his birthplace was at North Nibley is, however, rather doubtful. Two miles east from Wotton as the crow flies is **Ozleworth,** a place to be visited. A G.P.O. radio tower dominates the scene for many miles. Walkers are advised to take the rough lane along the southern side of the valley immediately below the town, and to return by the lane down the valley of the diminutive Avon to Wortley and thence along the hillside. Motorists follow the Stroud road for nearly 5 miles to the lane on the right leading down to Ozleworth. The road on the left is that to Dursley by Whiteway Hill (*see* p. 145).

**Ozleworth Church** is one of the most remarkable buildings in the country, consisting of a tall hexagonal tower to which have been added a chancel and a nave. The lower part of the tower was probably the fortified part of a hunting lodge, which stood at the centre of a roughly circular piece of ground. A small chancel was added, the tower serving as a nave, until the Norman nave was added, and the upper portion of the tower built. Except for a single deeply-splayed opening (a later insertion) high up on the south-west side the only windows in the tower are the six two-light typically Norman windows just under the eaves. The western arch, leading to the nave, is of Early English work—and extremely beautiful work it is, zigzag and chevron deeply undercut—while the south doorway is Norman, as is the blocked up doorway on the north side. The font is Norman with dog's tooth and nailhead moulding. The rood-loft stairs remain and in the east window is some old glass. The church is small, but is packed with details of interest, and is a place not to be missed.

There is a fine manor-house, **Newark Park** (National Trust), which was restored with the stone brought from Kingswood Abbey, after its destruction. An underground passage, part of which still remains, is locally thought to have led to Kingswood.

Neighbouring **Boxwell** derives its name from a great wood of box trees covering 40 acres. It is a pretty spot: one can imagine that even the unhappy Charles II, who came here in the course of his flight from Worcester, derived a sense of peace during his brief visit.

The head of the wooded valleys containing Lasborough, Boxwell and Ozleworth is close to **Newington Bagpath,** with an old mound, the site of an early castle, and church dating back in part to Saxon times. At Calcot Farm at the cross-roads on the Tetbury road is a fine old tithe barn. Over 40 yards long, and capable of holding 900 loads of corn, it dates from the time of Edward I, though it was partly burnt down in 1728.

Newington Bagpath is just below the Tetbury road, which passes through **Beverstone,** one of the South Cotswold villages which answers most clearly to the North Cotswold type: groups of stone-roofed cottages standing in gardens, a collection of stone barns, small but well-proportioned and with a worthy neighbour in the ruins of the moated castle built here in the thirteenth century (on the site of an earlier castle) by Maurice de Gaunt and again reconstructed a century later by the Lord Berkeley of those days. Like so many Cotswold scenes, this group looks sufficiently peaceful now, but in 1644 it wore a very different aspect, for the castle was besieged by a Parliamentary force, and was only taken after the governor had been captured and forced to tell Colonel Massey its weakest spot.

Hidden among trees beside the barns and castle, Beverstone Church is apt to be overlooked, but it has much to show. Originally Norman, it was restored in 1361. The fine south arcade and doorway are *c.* 1200, but the Berkeley Chapel was erected in the fourteenth century. Note that it is connected with the chancel by the large passage-squint under the rood-loft stairs. There is a well-carved stone pulpit, good windows with mouldings in the chancel, and an unusual roof.

## Tetbury

Tetbury is a picturesque town of wide streets with a spacious Market Hall (restored *c.* 1820)—now the Town Hall—standing on pillars in the centre of the town. It has a long history, evidenced by the burial mounds and Roman relics discovered in the neighbourhood. The Saxon name was given to the town by

Tetta, an abbess of Wimborne, who founded a monastery here. For centuries it was a flourishing centre of the wool trade; some of the fine houses built by the merchants still stand. One interesting building is the house in Long Street, dated 1677, now used as offices by the local Council.

Originally Norman, the church was entirely built in 1787, but the dominating spire and tower were reconstructed in 1890. The interior of the church is interesting for its unusual straight-backed box pews entered from narrow corridors, with slender pillars supporting the vaulted roof.

Three miles south-west of Tetbury is **Westonbirt,** a well-known public school for girls. Founded in 1928, the school occupies the mansion of the late Sir George Holford, situated in 500 acres of lovely parkland, where grow lovely and rare trees. The arboretum is open to visitors. There is a 9-hole golf course.

Some 6 miles south-east of Tetbury is the picturesque town of—

## Malmesbury

Access.—Bus from Bristol, Swindon, Cirencester, etc.
Early Closing.—Thursday.
Hotels.—*See* p. 11.
Licensing Hours.—10.30–2.30, 6–10.30; Sundays, 12–2, 7–10.30.
Population.—2,550.

Here is history enshrined in stone and story. Archaeologists and architects will find much to delight them. Roman history is obscure, Saxon well authenticated and Norman still in glad being in the rare beauty of the glorious remnant of the Abbey.

Nearby is the splendid **Market Cross.** Dating from the reign of Henry VII, it ranks with few similar crosses in the country and is one of the most ornate. The cross itself is not well defined, being, as in most cases, a central shaft surrounded by a shelter, and used for marketing on inclement days. Close inspection will, however, reveal its medieval architecture. It was restored in 1954. The central pinnacle is 40 feet from the ground.

A few yards west of the market cross is the fourteenth-century clock tower of the parish church with a peal of bells; opposite to this, where now a large mirror warns of approaching traffic, was the heavily guarded "local" gateway of the town, the "Salleporte". The *Old Bell Hotel* is built on the site of the twelfth-century castle which was erected north of the abbey and demolished in the thirteenth century.

South of the market cross the High Street, flanked by pleasant houses and picturesque inns, leads to **St. John's Bridge.** Near by, in Lower High Street stands the remaining portion of **St. John's Hospital.** In the thirteenth century this was the Hospital of St. John of Jerusalem, but it was later maintained in accordance with a seventeenth-century foundation the details of which are

155

set out on a stone tablet above what was evidently at one time the main entrance, though the arch has been part filled in. Behind this is the old Court Room of the principal burgesses and commoners, the former "borough council".

These things are of small account, however, compared with the principal feature of the town—the monastic church of—

## Malmesbury Abbey

Tragic in its maimed loveliness is Malmesbury Abbey Church. Built by Norman masons not merely as a place of worship but as a material expression of their religious exultation, it was sold for £1,500 at the Dissolution to "an exceeding riche clothiar", William Stumpe, who was so far unaware of the treasure which had fallen into his hands that some of it he used as workshops and other parts he pulled down. By way of forestalling possible local criticism he graciously gave permission for divine service to be performed in the nave, an astute move which seems to have been entirely successful. The Abbey was licensed as a parish church by Cranmer in 1541.

Even when the Normans arrived on the scene Malmesbury as a religious institution was old; in fact, it ranks with Canterbury as one of the significant sites in English church history.

Tradition affirms that a convent existed here as early as the sixth century, and Malmesbury as a religious foundation is dated back to the days of the ancient Celtic Church, before the coming of St. Augustine from Rome.

Malmesbury's recorded history, however, opens with the coming of Maeldub from Ireland, and the coming to Maeldub's priory of the youthful Aldhelm, here to acquire those rudiments of education and training which were to lead to his promotion first to headship of the Priory, as a mitred abbot, and later to the newly-formed Bishopric of Sherborne. Malmesbury, therefore, was not merely a fine Norman building; not merely the religious cradle of the saintly Aldhelm, but one of the early battlegrounds of English church history—and an important battleground at that.

Of all these things Stumpe may have known nothing and cared less; but one cannot overlook his allowing destruction of the priceless library, however much one may wish to overlook his action in setting up looms in "the little church joining the south side of the transept".

Nor was Stumpe the only culprit; for having acquired their parish church the townspeople seemed content to let it gradually fall into decay. For close on 300 years no attempt seems to have been made to repair, much less adorn, the building. As parts of the fabric fell, the stones were left lying—an opportunity not overlooked by local builders. When, at length, in 1823, it became necessary to avert disaster, no less a sum than £10,000 had to be called for (and money values were different a century ago); and even then only half that sum was subscribed and only half the work could be done, and what was done was done in a makeshift manner. The floor of the nave, for example, instead of being properly repaired was covered with a false floor, laid on joists which were let into holes cut in the walls and entirely covering the bases of the Norman pillars. Other mistakes were made, and to those more responsible folk who came after the task must have seemed wellnigh hopeless: a constant series of weaknesses developing in the building, to repair which there was all too little money. The last great restoration was begun in 1927. Later, in 1934, it was found that the vaulting over the new choir stalls was in imminent danger of falling, and a year later the great north arch of the fallen central tower, which supports, like a flying buttress, the east end of the Abbey Church as it now stands, was found to be in such a precarious state that immediate steps had to be taken to save it and the load it carries—a task entailing an additional cost of £300. Fortunately during the past few years this great and lovely fragment has received the care of which it has so long been starved, and though no amount of skill can cloak the destruction and the errors of earlier days one places one's contribution in the collecting-box with the assurance that one is helping good and necessary work.

The original church consisted of a nave of nine bays, transepts with eastern chapels, a massive central tower and another at the west end, and at the east end a long choir beyond which was a Lady Chapel. To the north of the nave lay the great Cloister and to the east of that the Chapter House, and north of these again were the domestic quarters of the monks. Old Leland tells us that the church was "a righte magnificent thing, with two steeples . . . a marke to all the countrie about." The steeples are steeples no more, only the lower part of the western tower remaining and the northern arch of the central tower. But the flying buttresses with their tall pinnacles make a fine show as they lead the eye from the pierced parapet of the aisle walls to where the nave walls also terminate in pierced parapets, so that as one approaches the South Porch the whole effect—perpendicular lines of pinnacles contrasted with the rounded arch of the dark and almost cavernous south porch—is one of great grandeur.

Had everything else fallen, Malmesbury would still be worth visiting for the sake of its **South Porch**, certainly the finest example of Norman work left in this country. The entrance arch has eight orders, all richly carved, alternately with leaves and foliage and with scriptural and other subjects. The whole conception and execution are far richer than any other similar arch in Britain, and in view of the neglect which has befallen the remainder of the building it is remarkable that so much of the carving is still decipherable. The carvings are mostly of Biblical incidents. Those of the Apostles which flank the sides of the inner porch are unique examples of exquisite work.

By the inner door, with its three orders of carvings and its finely carved tympanum, we enter the south aisle of the church and in a few paces have a glimpse of the former majesty of the building—but only a glimpse, for there are but six bays left: all eastward is cut off by a blank wall which cannot be cloaked by even the most skilful decoration. Note the thickness of the nave pillars, their bases sadly maltreated when the false floor was laid in 1823. And above the nave arcade see the triforium and the clerestory, and imagine the spectacle when this grand building carried so much farther eastward. But the blank wall puts an abrupt end to the vista. At the eastern end of the aisles are portions of the stone screen which originally stretched right across the church, and projecting from the south triforium wall of the nave is what was probably a watching loft used by the Sacristan when guarding the abbey treasures.

The treasures of the Abbey were considerable, and included a piece of the True Cross, a Thorn from the Crown of Thorns and the bones of St. Aldhelm, who when he died in 705 was buried here. With such wealth of relics it can well be believed that the stream of pilgrims was heavy and unceasing and the fame of Malmesbury great and widespread. The Parvise, or Porch Room, has some beautiful and valuable manuscripts. There is a "Breeches" Bible and a Saxon coin minted in Malmesbury, several pictures, pewter flagons, and some ancient musical instruments used when organs had not come into general use.

In the north aisle is the monument of King Athelstan. It is of early fourteenth-century date and was moved from the choir at the Dissolution. The King's head, and that of the lion at his feet, were cut off by Parliamentarian soldiers but replaced (from memory) by a local sculptor at the Restoration.

From Malmesbury it is 15 miles to Stroud, which with its immediate neighbourhood is described on pp. 137–146.

# Index

*Where more than one reference is given, the first is the principal.*

159

# INDEX